THE OXFORD WORC & WOLVERHAMPTON RAILWAY

In the dying days of steam but still managing to look respectable, 7032 "Denbigh Castle" with a westbound local near Campden, April 1963.
(T.E.Williams, National Railway Museum)

John Boynton

A selection of tickets from the collection of Robert Pearson.

Ivatt 2-6-2T No.41203 stands at Kidderminster in July 1962 with a train for Shrewsbury, which will travel 'wrong road' for the short distance to the junction of the Severn Valley line. There is much of interest here, including the ornate station building, two ex-GWR travelling safes, pigeon baskets, a clutter of carpets in transit, a pannier tank waiting in the siding with another southbound train, and the older lad on the right whose pose says - unconvincingly - 'I do have some street cred'.

(A.W.V.Mace, Mile Post 92^{1}/$_{2}$, Roger Carpenter collection)

CONTENTS

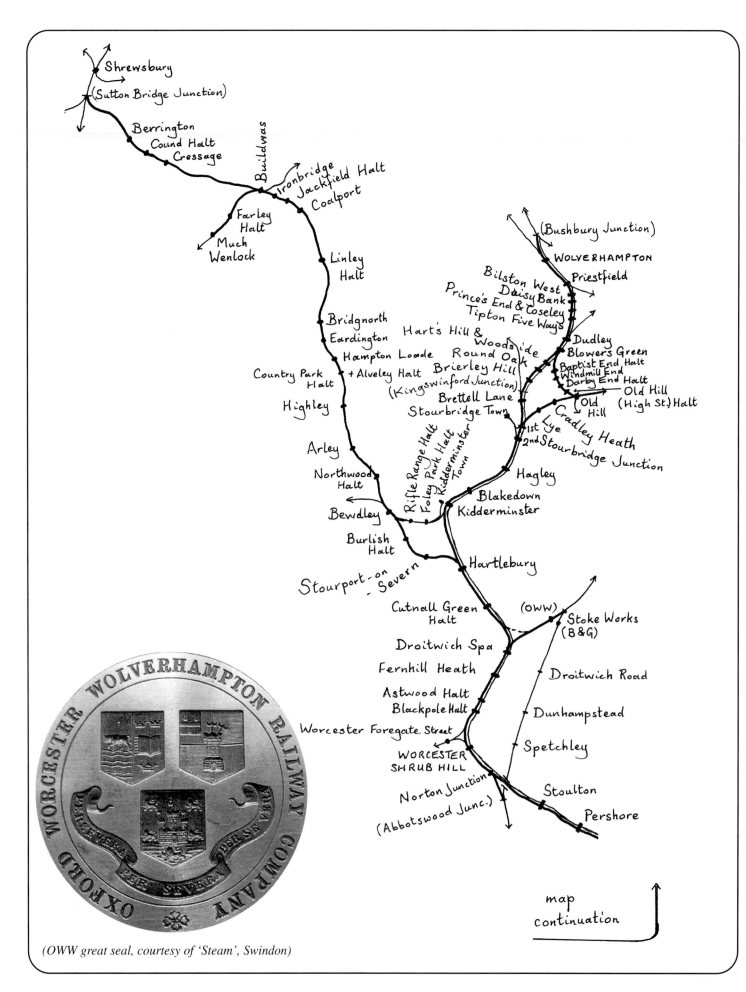

Shrewsbury

(Sutton Bridge Junction)

Berrington
Cound Halt
Cressage

Buildwas

Ironbridge
Jackfield Halt
Coalport

Farley
Halt

Much
Wenlock

Linley
Halt

Bridgnorth
Eardington

Hampton Loade
+ Alveley Halt

Country Park
Halt

Highley

Arley

Northwood
Halt

Bewdley

Burlish
Halt

Stourport-on-Severn

Rifle Range Halt
Foley Park Halt
Kidderminster Town

(Bushbury Junction)

WOLVERHAMPTON

Priestfield

Bilston West
Daisy Bank
Prince's End & Coseley
Tipton Five Ways

Hart's Hill &
Woodside
Round Oak
Brierley Hill
(Kingswinford Junction)

Brettell Lane
Stourbridge Town

Dudley
Blowers Green
Baptist End Halt
Windmill End
Darby End Halt
Old Hill
(High St.) Halt

Old
Hill

Cradley Heath

1st Lye
2nd Stourbridge Junction

Hagley

Blakedown

Kidderminster

Hartlebury

Cutnall Green
Halt

(OWW)

Stoke Works
(B & G)

Droitwich Spa

Fernhill Heath

Astwood Halt
Blackpole Halt

Worcester Foregate Street

WORCESTER
SHRUB HILL

Norton Junction

(Abbotswood Junc.)

Droitwich Road

Dunhampstead

Spetchley

Stoulton

Pershore

map
continuation

4

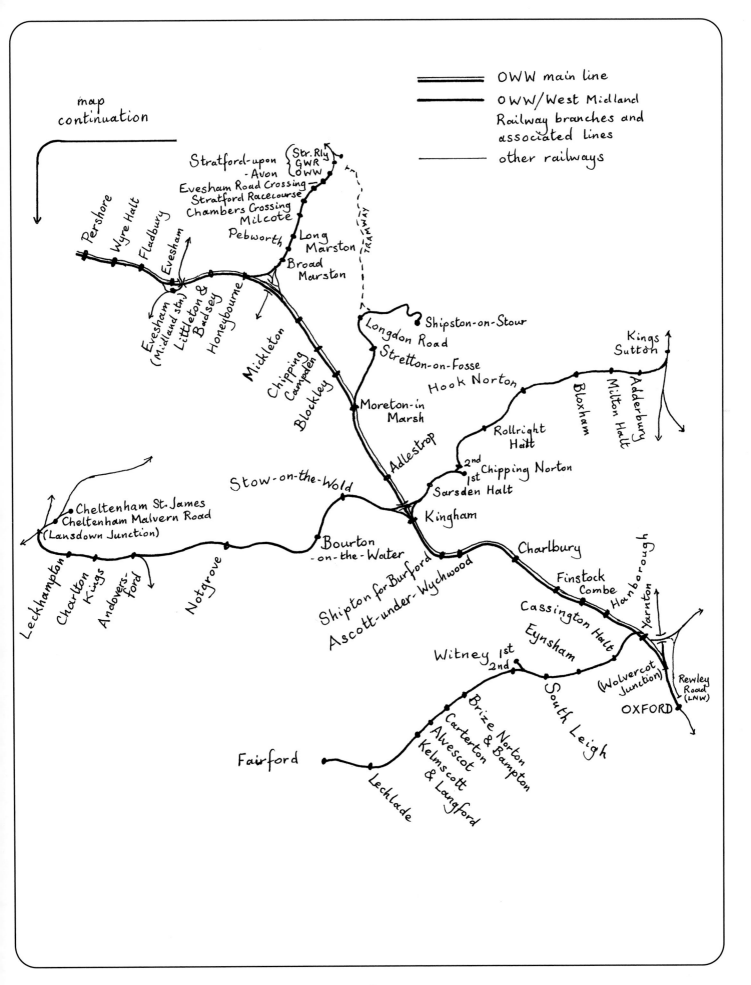

map continuation

OWW main line

OWW/West Midland Railway branches and associated lines

other railways

Stratford-upon-Avon — Str. Rly / GWR / OWW

Evesham Road Crossing — Stratford Racecourse

Chambers Crossing

Milcote

Pebworth

Long Marston

Broad Marston

TRAMWAY

Pershore

Wyre Halt

Fladbury

Evesham

Evesham (Midland stn.)

Littleton & Badsey

Honeybourne

Mickleton

Chipping Campden

Blockley

Shipston-on-Stour

Longdon Road

Stretton-on-Fosse

Hook Norton

Moreton-in-Marsh

Adlestrop

Kings Sutton

Adderbury

Milton Halt

Bloxham

Rollright Halt

2nd Chipping Norton

1st

Sarsden Halt

Stow-on-the-Wold

Kingham

Cheltenham St. James

Cheltenham Malvern Road

(Lansdown Junction)

Leckhampton

Charlton Kings

Andoversford

Notgrove

Bourton-on-the-Water

Shipton for Burford

Ascott-under-Wychwood

Charlbury

Finstock Combe

Cassington Halt

Eynsham

Hanborough

Yarnton

(Wolvercot Junction)

Rewley Road (LNW)

OXFORD

Witney 1st

2nd

South Leigh

Brize Norton & Bampton

Carterton

Alvescot

Kelmscott & Langford

Fairford

Lechlade

5

INTRODUCTION

The Oxford Worcester & Wolverhampton Railway has had a bad press almost from the beginning, the words 'old worse and worse' slipping all too easily from the lips. It certainly had problems, some of its own making, but it is doubtful if the OWW was any worse than many other railways during the 1850s. After a shaky start, and with limited finances, it managed to run a successful train service. Before it was taken over by the Great Western Railway in 1863 it had grown, by amalgamation with two smaller companies, into the West Midland Railway, and had also promoted several important branch lines, including the Severn Valley Railway.

The main line remained intact until 1962, since when the OWW has enjoyed mixed fortunes. The decline experienced in the 1960s continued into the 70s, with the singling of long sections of track, the loss of a considerable amount of freight and a sharp reduction in some passenger services.

Happily, there has been a revival in fortune since that time; cuts have been restored, time-tables improved and new rolling stock introduced. There are now more passenger services than ever before - over the part of the line, south of Stourbridge, that still carries them. Freight has fared less well, although there is hope that the line between Round Oak and Dudley will be reopened for freight and passenger traffic at some point in the future.

It came as a pleasant surprise to discover that Railtrack has a sense of history. Some of the bridges along the line now display, above their mileage markers, the newly stencilled initials 'OWW'.

John Boynton
2002

CHAPTER ONE : PROMOTION and CONSTRUCTION

[Diary : Promotion : Double Dealing and Other Difficulties : Reading the Riot Act : Brunel's Influence : The London Extension : David Joy]

Diary

1840
24th June : Worcester's first station opened at Spetchley.
1844
22nd & 29th May : OWW prospectus published in the "Wolverhampton Chronicle".
1845
4th August : Act of Parliament passed for building of OWW.
1846
18th August : Regulations of Gauges Act limits spread of broad gauge.
1848
14th August : Act determining that Wolverhampton (later known as Low Level) would be a joint station.

1850
5th October : First section of OWW opened, Abbotswood Junction-Worcester Shrub Hill. Line worked by the Midland Railway by special agreement.
1851
20th-23rd July : 'Battle of Mickleton' during the construction of Campden Tunnel.
1852
18th February : OWW opened, Worcester - Droitwich and Stoke Works. New stations at Fearnhill Heath, Droitwich and Stoke Works. Trains continued to be worked by the Midland.
28th February : Completion of Hoobrook Viaduct, Kidderminster.
19th April : David Joy takes up his appointment.

Promotion

The years between August 1845, when the Oxford Worcester & Wolverhampton Railway was sanctioned by Act of Parliament, and April 1854, when it was completed, were bedevilled by two major problems, money and width. Money, or the lack of it, still casts a shadow over this country's railways in the twenty-first century but width, or the gauge of the track, is no longer an issue. Early in the railway era most lines were built to a gauge of 4 feet 8½ inches (1.435metres), although no one now quite knows why. Most engineers were content to adopt this gauge as standard.

In 1833 Isambard Kingdon Brunel, the 27-year-old son of a French refugee father and English mother was given the task of constructing a line linking London with Bristol. One of the greatest engineers of any century, he set to work with gusto. The Great Western main line remains a superb example of civil engineering, known to railwaymen as 'Brunel's billiard table'. What set it apart from all other lines - typical of Brunel's innovative style and his desire always to start any new project free of pre-conceptions - was the gauge of the track. At 7 feet (2.134 metres) it was broader than any other. He was right to think it better suited than the 4' 8½" gauge for smooth fast running, both for his own age and into the future. This fact continued to be acknowledged many times long after the broad gauge became extinct, even by those who would not describe themselves as friends of the Great Western, for example - *"It is generally admitted now that the broad gauge was perhaps the more efficient."* ('History of the London & North Western Railway, W.L.Steel, pub.1914). The tragedy was that Brunel entered the arena too late; by 1844 there were 2175 miles of railway in

The first new locomotive delivered to the OWW, No.1 "Hawthorn", photographed as No.171 in GWR ownership. When new it took a passenger train from Kidderminster to Stourbridge in a little under nine minutes. It was scrapped in 1885.

(National Railway Museum)

Britain, of which only 274 were broad gauge (these figures vary slightly, according to the source consulted). If this country were to adopt one gauge as standard - imperative for ease of trade and travel - it was already obvious which it would be.

1844 was also the year in which the Oxford Worcester & Wolverhampton Railway company (OWW) was formed. It was backed by the Great Western. The London & North Western Railway, which provided what was still the only rail link between London and the West Midlands, did not welcome the prospect of competition from either the Great Western or OWW. The OWW itself was supposed to be built to the broad gauge but, in the event, no revenue earning broad gauge train ever ran over it …

There were at least three earlier schemes for a railway between Oxford and Worcester. While Brunel was busy with the Great Western main line he was also being commissioned to engineer other routes. According to L.T.C.Rolt's 1957 biography 'Isambard Kingdom Brunel', his diary entry for 14th April 1836 reads, *"I have added to my stock in trade the Plymouth Railway, the Oxford branch and today somewhat against my will the Worcester & Oxford.* (an early scheme, not built) *Here's another £2,500,000 of capital - I may say £8,000,000 and really all very likely to go on. And what is satisfactory all reflecting credit upon me and most of them almost forced upon me …Really my business is something extraordinary"*.

An Oxford 'branch' from Didcot opened in 1844, ending in a temporary terminus a little to the south of the present station. It was never meant to be just a branch, but was intended as the first stage of broad gauge expansion to the West Midlands and beyond. It was also to become the starting point for another route to the West Midlands, to Wolverhampton via Worcester.

Worcester had begun to feel the benefits of rail travel earlier, when the Birmingham and Gloucester Railway (B&G) opened in 1840. The line passes to the east of Worcester and a station was provided at Spetchley, four miles from the city centre on the road to Alcester. Every train was met by a coach from the Crown Inn, Broad Street, where through tickets were issued, valid for coach and train. The coach could accommodate 15 passengers and the journey took half an hour. Spetchley was also a goods station, (finally closing in this capacity on 1st January 1961) and the means for speeding up the city's mails. The B&G was awarded a Post Office contract and the first mail trains ran, calling at Spetchley, on 14th January 1841.

The Spetchley coach link was not seen as a permanent way to serve the city; the railway had to come closer. Other places were thinking the same. By 1838, courtesy of the London & Birmingham (L&B) and Grand Junction (GJ) railways, Birmingham, Wolverhampton and a few Black Country towns had access to rail travel - to London, Manchester and Liverpool. There were problems from the outset. The GJ had remotely sited stations serving Wolverhampton (at Wednesfield Heath), Walsall (at Bescot) and West Bromwich (at Newton Road). The line opened in 1837 but the final mile in Birmingham could not open until completion of Lawley Street viaduct in January 1839. Only then could there be a smooth interchange of passengers and freight between the adjoining GJ and L&B stations at Curzon Street.

Some Black Country manufacturers were already looking for something better. When it came to transporting their products, particularly to London, their introduction to railways had not been smooth. They alleged that the L&B was charging excessive rates for an unreliable service, although no one suggested reverting to road or canal. Most industries thrive or perish with the stimulus of competition so, in discussing the shortcomings of the new railway, it was inevitable that the idea of an alternative route to London would emerge. Expanding industrial communities within the Black Country, such as Bilston, Tipton and Brierley Hill, and two towns to the south - Stourbridge and Kidderminster - readily appreciated the need to be rail-connected. Stourbridge in particular needed no lessons in the benefits of rail. The three mile long Shutt End Railway had been linking the Earl of Dudley's coal mines in Pensnett with the Staffordshire & Worcestershire Canal since 1829. Pride of the line was "Agenoria", a locomotive designed and built at Stourbridge by John Urpeth Rastrick, and now at the National Railway Museum, York.

Stourbridge and Kidderminster had, like Worcester, already been by-passed by the Birmingham & Gloucester Railway. It had intended to serve Stourbridge and Kidderminster before discovering that land on the less contentious and more direct route via Bromsgrove would be cheaper to buy up. After 1840 it was no longer the complete lack of a railway that spurred people into action, but rather the presence of a railway at one remove. Coach links with the new line, from Worcester, Droitwich and Stourbridge, could only be second best. Another railway was required, linking Stourbridge and Kidderminster to the north with the biggest town in the Black Country - Wolverhampton - and to the south with Worcester, then across rail-less country to Oxford, where the Great Western 'branch' would give access to London. If only it were that simple …

The Great Western, meanwhile, was busy planning extensions of its broad gauge lines, westwards to Devon, Cornwall and South Wales, north from Oxford to Birmingham and the West Midlands, then on to Merseyside. The intended railway from Oxford to Worcester and Wolverhampton lay entirely within what the GWR hoped would soon be its territory. Naturally the Great Western Board of Directors was 'interested' in the new line, but was this the benevolent interest of a senior colleague, or that of a bird of prey surveying its next meal? On the other hand, would the promoters of the new line be seeking a genuine and mutually beneficial working relationship with the GWR, or were they looking for an easy ride at that company's expense? In any event, by September 1844 the promoters of the OWW felt able to finalise an agreement with the GWR whereby the Great Western would lease the OWW for 999 years (until September 2843).

Brunel had surveyed the route and estimated the total cost at £1½ million. This figure, for about ninety miles of double track main line, was to prove inadequate. The capital of the OWW was fixed at that sum and the GWR agreed to pay a rent of 3½% on the capital, plus half the profits. This seemed to offer potential investors a reasonable return for their money. Interest in the OWW grew as public meetings were held along its intended route. At one such, in Worcester's Guildhall, a Stourbridge banker, Francis Rufford, proclaimed the advantages of the OWW adopting the broad gauge, because of the higher speeds and smoother running of the trains, and the heavier and larger loads that could be carried. He also commended the courteous dealings the OWW had already had with the GWR, suggesting that they should act upon that company's advice and recommendations. Rufford subsequently became Chairman of the OWW.

The OWW Prospectus was published in the "Wolverhampton Chronicle" on 22nd and 29th May 1844. Brunel was to be Engineer. Shares cost £50 each, secured by a £5 deposit. Among the many railway schemes then being proposed, *there is not one which is entitled, both on public and private grounds, to more favourable consideration than the project mentioned at the head of this prospectus, calculated as it is to benefit one of the most important mineral and manufacturing districts in the kingdom, and at the same time to afford to its proprietors a rate of remuneration equal to that which is yielded by the most successful undertakings now in operation*.

The northern end was to *branch out of the Grand Junction Railway … at the station near the important manufacturing town of Wolverhampton*. Stourbridge was *principally engaged in the manufacture of iron, glass, firebricks, etc, which will be largely benefited by the proposed measure*. As for the carpet factories of Kidderminster, *the principal part of their productions is sent to London for sale*. The salt industry at Droitwich and Stoke Works already consumed *not less than 100,000 tons of coal per annum, and if brought into immediate connexion with the extensive coalfield through which this railway will pass, the consumption will no doubt be materially increased*. With a population of 27,000, Worcester was *an important market for agricultural produce, hops, fruit, cider, etc. as well as the principal seat of the glove and porcelain manufactures of the kingdom. From Worcester ..... to Oxford the district is principally agricultural, but the country to be traversed is of the easiest description*, so much so that the promoters did not see the need for any tunnel between Worcester and Oxford. The Prospectus concluded, *Four Directors of the Great Western Railway will act on the committee of management, which is in itself a guarantee for the bona fide of the undertaking …* It was signed by those directors, plus thirty-one men from whose number a committee of management would be formed. They included the mayors of Worcester and Evesham, Francis Rufford, two Kidderminster carpet manufacturers and seven clay and ironmasters from Stourbridge.

Early in 1845 the Bill for the OWW was presented to Parliament. It had to join a very long queue, as the country was in the grip of the so-called Railway Mania. Now that railways were seen as 'A Good Thing', not least by City financiers, who had shown no previous interest, there was an explosion of enthusiasm from people who wanted either to build or invest in them. Many important lines were authorised during this period of chaotic energy, including the OWW. As the Mania grew, the proliferation of fanciful and downright fraudulent schemes, alongside the more rational proposals, fuelled a huge speculative bubble which rapidly ballooned out of control. The bubble had burst before the end of 1846, causing the abandonment of most schemes and the ruin of countless small investors.

The fact that the OWW was proposed as a broad gauge line was an added dimension at a time when some MPs were becoming more aware of the obvious - that all lines should be of one gauge. Railway Bills had to be lodged with the Railways Department of the Board of Trade whose President was William Gladstone. He made no secret of his disapproval of the broad gauge OWW. He preferred a Bill, sponsored by the London & Birmingham, for a line to Worcester and Wolverhampton, which would leave the L&B at Tring and pass through Banbury and Evesham. When the OWW Bill reached the Committee stage in the Commons it was examined minutely. During a thirty day hearing, a total of 12,148 questions were put to over one hundred witnesses. Despite this war of words, which would no doubt have provided some very interesting soundbites had radio and television existed, the Committee rejected the L&B line and reported in favour of the OWW. The Bill was subsequently passed by the Commons by 247 votes to 113 in its third and final reading there on 24th June 1845.

"From Worcester . . . to Oxford the district is principally agricultural . . ."

Rural, tranquil, delightful, but hopelessly uneconomic. Class 2251 0-6-0 freight loco No.2246 (a 1930 design), trundles its single Hawksworth coach gently past the blossom at Aston Magna, two miles from its destination, with the 5.50pm Honeybourne to Moreton-in-Marsh, 25th May 1963. The train displays the light engine headcode! *(Michael Mensing)*

"Important mineral and manufacturing districts" could also appear rural . . .

Six weeks before closure of the northern end of the OWW to passengers, ex-GWR 2-6-2T No.4179 enters Tipton Five Ways with the 5.27pm Stourbridge Junction-Wolverhampton Low Level, 16th June 1962. *(G.E.S.Parker, Kidderminster Railway Museum)*

This proved too bitter a pill for Richard Cobden, a radical MP and strong supporter of a uniform national railway gauge. The following day he moved a resolution proposing that a Royal Commission be set up to investigate the gauge question. His resolution was unopposed and the Commission began work on 9th July. It reported in February 1846 in favour of the 4' 8½" gauge. The Regulation of Gauges Act, of 18th August 1846, effectively prevented further spread of the broad gauge. There is a double irony here - by voting in favour of the broad gauge OWW, the House of Commons unwittingly signed the death warrant for the broad gauge; the OWW was built with broad gauge rails throughout but never had a broad gauge train service.

The OWW Bill successfully negotiated the House of Lords, finally becoming an Act on receiving Queen Victoria's signature - the Royal Assent - on 4th August 1845. A key clause (no.38) stated:-

"And be it enacted, That the said Railway, Branch Railways, and Works, shall be constructed and completed in all respects to the satisfaction of the engineer, for the time being, to the Great Western Railway Company, and the said Railway shall be formed of such a gauge, and according to such mode of construction, as will admit of the same being worked continuously with the said Great Western Railway."

No room for doubt, this was to be a broad gauge line. The junction at Wolverhampton, with the Grand Junction line, was to be at Bushbury. A spur at Abbotswood and a link line between Droitwich and Stoke Works would put Worcester on a loop off the Birmingham & Gloucester main line. The loop was to be mixed gauge, like the rest of the OWW north of Worcester because the OWW was required to lay down (clause 44) *"on the main line between the said Birmingham & Gloucester and Grand Junction Railways such additional rails adapted to the gauge of (those) Railways"*. However, the line between Oxford (Wolvercot Junction) and Worcester (Abbotswood junction) was intended as broad gauge only. There was to be a freight branch to the canal basin at Tipton, and another at Kingswinford. At Round Oak, the OWW was to cross the Pensnett line, an extension of the Shutt End Railway. This coal line was slow, primitive and devoid of passengers. However it was there first and had been financed by a member of the nobility, the Earl of Dudley. Therefore it was, by implication, much more important than a mere double track main line with broad gauge potential. The OWW was to be constructed (clause 54) *"so as to pass on a level across the Pensnett Railway, and so as not to alter the intended line of the Pensnett Railway as now being made, without the consent of the said William Baron Ward in writing first had and obtained."*

The Great Western was empowered to nominate six of the OWW's sixteen directors and to complete construction should the OWW fail to do so. The Act (clause 50) allowed five years for completion. It took almost nine.

Worcester was 57 miles from Oxford and 33½ miles from Wolverhampton. The biggest place en route, it was the logical site for the OWW headquarters. The B&G was to become part of the Midland Railway in 1846. Its main line expresses would serve Worcester as soon as the loop opened, giving direct access to places well beyond the OWW, such as Birmingham, Bristol and Derby. (By March 1852 the Midland was advertising new connections with other companies, placing Edinburgh just 11 hours 2 minutes from Worcester, *"the value of this to persons engaged in business or commerce can hardly be over rated"*). As the Midland was an important player in Worcester, Shrub Hill was a joint OWW/Midland station. It remained in the hands of these companies and their successors - GWR/LMS - until nationalisation in 1948.

During the passage of the OWW Bill through Parliament, the GWR was promoting other schemes to expand into the Midlands and beyond, using Oxford as a bridgehead. A Bill was presented for a nominally independent broad gauge Oxford & Rugby Railway (O&R), via Banbury. The O&R had just as stormy a passage through Parliament as the OWW, again because of the gauge, although it, too, received the Royal Assent, on the same day, with the proviso that it should be of mixed gauge. The OWW itself was not to connect directly with the Great Western at Oxford, but with the Oxford & Rugby at Wolvercot Junction, north of the city.

The GWR quickly realised that, despite Parliamentary approval, building a line to Rugby would unleash an unprecedented railway 'war'. Apart from the GWR, there were just two important railway companies in the country during the 1840s, the London & North Western (formed of the L&B, GJ and Manchester & Birmingham railways in 1846) and the Midland (formed 1844). The LNWR lines from Euston to Birmingham and north-west England passed through Rugby. The Midland, too, was developing a network to the north, centred on Derby. Neither would tolerate a broad gauge intrusion into 'their' territory. During the autumn of 1845 the Gauge Commission was busily deliberating. Like everyone else, the GWR directors knew what it would say but, unwilling to abandon expansion of the broad gauge just yet, they pointed the Rugby end of their new route in another more congenial direction, free of controversial junctions with other lines.

After absorbing the Oxford & Rugby in May 1846, the GWR promoted a new route involving three more nominally independent companies. The Birmingham & Oxford Junction Railway (B&O) would leave the O&R at Fenny Compton and continue to Birmingham, via Leamington. The route continued through a town centre station at Snow Hill on the tracks of the Birmingham Extension Railway. The Birmingham Wolverhampton & Dudley Railway would complete the route to Wolverhampton. The line in this form was sanctioned by Act of Parliament on 3rd August 1846, just fifteen days before the Regulation of Gauges Act. The Oxford & Rugby north of Fenny Compton was never built. The idea of doing so was abandoned in 1849.

Double Dealing and Other Difficulties

The new GWR-sponsored line to Wolverhampton via Birmingham was in direct competition with the OWW. However, the OWW Chairman, Francis Rufford, with two fellow directors, also became directors of the new route's companies. The Birmingham Wolverhampton & Dudley (BW&D) had an authorised capital of £700,000, of which the OWW contributed the largest single sum, £100,000. This was not as odd as it might seem, because the "& Dudley" in the BW&D's name referred to a link with the OWW, at Dudley, which would give the OWW easy access to Birmingham (A link eventually opened in 1866, by which time the OWW was part of the Great Western.)

The Railway Mania had consequences which Brunel had not foreseen when calculating the £1½ million cost of the OWW, Manpower and materials were both in demand, commanding high prices and affecting costs even before construction began. The OWW was leased to the Great Western, at a rate fixed at £52,000 per year in 1844. Francis Rufford, Chairman, wrote to Charles Russell, GWR Chairman, asking for an increase in this rate, without mentioning a figure. In effect, he wanted a blank cheque. Russell refused to consider it without a written figure and he also called on Brunel to give a revised estimate for the likely cost of the line. Brunel produced a figure of £2½ million. The GWR Directors agreed that this was to be the maximum amount they

A Round Oak steelworks locomotive, "Duchess of Gloucester", travelling north, crosses the OWW main line on the Pensnett Railway, about 1960.   *(Ned Williams collection)*

Ex-LMS Stanier 4-6-0 5MT No.44829 heads north past Round Oak Steelworks with a Tavistock-Crewe train, mainly china clay. Seen from Round Oak North signal box, c.1958.   *(Ned Williams collection)*

could guarantee. But there were no written formalities, just a 'gentlemen's agreement'. The OWW Directors published Rufford's report, which stated that the guarantee was extended *"to such a sum as shall appear to them"* (the GWR Directors) *"as necessary for completion of the said railway"* . It failed to mention the upper limit of £2½ million, implying that the Great Western would complete the line whatever the cost. Rufford had been economical with the truth, yet although the GWR Directors were aware of this, they made no effort, at this stage, to get him to admit it.

By the beginning of 1847 about 2,800 navvies were busy constructing the line. The earthworks were beginning to take shape along much of the route. OWW funds, always tight, were beginning to run low. In August that year the OWW Directors asked the Great Western for an increase in payment on capital interest, which was refused. Even if relations between the OWW and GWR had been excellent at this point, the likely response would probably have been the same, as the country was experiencing major financial convulsions following the repeal of the Corn Laws in 1846. (The Corn Laws dated from 1804 and protected English farmers from economic reality by imposing a heavy duty on imported grain.) Many banks went out of business as the idea and then the practice of free trade took painful root. Economies were urgently needed on the OWW, as everywhere. Brunel thought that Worcester-Wolverhampton was the less important part of the line, so he decided that construction north of Worcester must cease. Work stopped, causing misery to the men - and their families - who were laid off. There was no welfare system, no redundancy money, no giro slip, only the charity of others at best or the threat of the workhouse at worst. The halving of the price of bread during the year, thanks to the repeal of the Corn Laws, was but small comfort. As on all lines then under construction, some navvies were Irish, recently come 'over the water' to escape the potato famine. To find themselves destitute for a second time within months was particularly harsh.

The directors of both companies were held to account by shareholders at their 1847 annual general meetings. The Great Western was criticised for the lack of a proper written agreement while at the OWW meeting, held soon afterwards, the lack of funds and the absence of construction made it clear what a poor investment the OWW had become, far removed from the flourishing railway promised in the Prospectus. Finances were exhausted, so work stopped on the southern part of the line too.

1847 had been a bad year; 1848 was worse. It started well enough, with the OWW Directors proposing an alteration to the route into Wolverhampton. Rather than connect just with the Grand Junction line, on the edge of the town at Wednesfield Heath, it made more sense to have a joint station in the town centre, to be shared between the OWW, Birmingham Wolverhampton & Dudley and a third company, the Shrewsbury & Birmingham. There would still be a connection with the Grand Junction, near Bushbury. The OWW and BW&D tracks would combine on their final approach to Wolverhampton, coming together at Priestfield. Parliamentary powers were sought to give these amendments legal authority, and they were granted by an Act of 14th August 1848, which also gave the OWW powers to raise an extra £1 million by issuing preference shares. However, riots in Paris in February that year had flowered into a full-blooded revolution which sparked popular unrest throughout much of Europe. Months of uncertainty brought normal life to a standstill. England was spared revolution but trade, recovering from the previous year's

financial crisis, was briefly plunged into recession once more. In such a climate there was no hope of construction starting again on the OWW and no prospect of rescue by the Great Western. This was confirmed in November 1848 when the Chairman, Charles Russell, finally reacted to the OWW statement of February 1846, which had implied that the GWR would underwrite OWW finances, come what may. Russell declined to have any communication with the OWW until they publicly acknowledged the limits of the financial guarantee. This they did in February 1849, at the same time announcing to shareholders that any interest on paid-up capital they might be expecting would be 'postponed'.

Eying their potential cash returns, and sensing that 'postponed' meant 'cancelled', the shareholders organised an emergency meeting in June 1849, establishing from among their number a Committee of Investigation. It quickly reported that an extra £1½ million would be required for the line to be completed. The Committee indicated that when work did start, priority should be given to constructing the line between Abbotswood (junction with the Birmingham-Gloucester line near Worcester) through Stourbridge and Dudley to Tipton. The line should be standard gauge only and should connect, by a previously unplanned link at Tipton, with the LNWR Birmingham New St.-Wolverhampton line then under construction. None of this had any official or legal basis, it strained relations with the GWR further and the Committee gave no clue as to how funds might be raised. The posturings of the Committee did at least attract the attention of an official body with some authority, the Commissioners of Railways, who directed Captain Simmons of the Railways Department at the Board of Trade to investigate. His report, dated 27th November 1849, described the state of the line. It was virtually complete between Tipton and Dudley, also between Stourbridge and Evesham. Work was less advanced beyond Evesham, especially between Shipton and Wolvercot Junction. Some sections of line were *"nearly ready for opening, with the exceptions of the stations and the permanent way not being laid"*. That sounds absurd, but most construction for a new railway consists of earthworks and formation. Laying the track on a prepared base is usually straightforward.

The 1845 Act empowered the Great Western to complete the line should the OWW be unable to do so. In January 1850 the Commissioners formally ordered the GWR to complete the line. The Great Western was busy constructing its own route between Oxford and Wolverhampton, via Birmingham, and it saw the OWW as an increasingly difficult wayward child. The order was ignored; 'empowered' was not going to be interpreted as 'compelled'. As this became apparent the corporations of Worcester, Evesham, Droitwich and Kidderminster jointly petitioned the Attorney General to begin legal proceedings against the GWR, but he took no action. This attempt to force the Great Western to complete the line ended in April 1851, when the Commissioners dropped their formal order because, at long last, extra capital had been raised and work had restarted, of which more later ...

The first section of the OWW had actually opened earlier, in 1850, when the national economy was recovering rapidly and entering a prolonged period of growth. At this time - *"the national output of iron was greater than that of the rest of the world put together ... coal output was two-thirds, and cotton cloth more than half, that of total world output"* ('A Social History of England', Asa Briggs, pub.1994).

Worcester Shrub Hill was a joint station from 1850 until 1948. Ex-Midland 4-4-0 No.40332 (Class 2P) enters with the 4.35pm Birmingham New Street-Gloucester, 27th May 1957. This locomotive was built at Derby in 1882, where it was rebuilt in 1910.

(John Edgington)

The Midland Railway was keen to serve Worcester direct, rather than via Spetchley. The company reached an agreement with the OWW to lay standard gauge track between Abbotswood Junction and Shrub Hill and - prior to completion of other sections of the OWW - to work the line. Track was laid during the summer and the train service began on 5th October 1850. The previous day's "Berrow's Journal" eagerly anticipated the event:- *"Tomorrow (Saturday) we people of Worcester shall be able to get into a railway carriage at our own doors and travel to the metropolis without the interposition of any other conveyance, and in consideration of the thing actually being affected, we will endeavour to forget that we have had to wait until the year 1850 before we could do so, and try to forget all those years of torture we have sustained in the joltings, dust, discomfort and delays of the Spetchley omnibus route.... The first passenger train will start ... tomorrow morning at 7.55 .... Everything connected with the single line of rails is now in readiness, but the company have permission to run only one engine until the second line shall be completed, which is expected to be in about a week. The station is also in a very forward state, and if not quite finished by tomorrow, will afford sufficient accommodation for the transaction of business and issue of tickets."*

There were five trains to Bristol and six to Birmingham. The Birmingham trains reversed at Abbotswood Junction. The Shrub Hill-Birmingham Curzon Street journey took over two hours. The first stop north of Spetchley, as it had been since 1840, was a wayside station called Droitwich Road, where trains were met by coaches for the three mile journey into that town.

That same year, 1850, the OWW was able to issue the £1 million worth of preference shares authorised in 1848. The prospect of money generated hopes for more money and fuelled the desire for a more independent railway. Some pro-Great Western Directors were 'resigned' at the end of 1850 and a group of active shareholders gathered enough support for a Special Shareholders' Meeting, which was convened in Worcester in January 1851. Francis Rufford, rather than ride a tiger which he no longer felt able or willing to control, vacated the Chair, never to reclaim it. His place was taken by Lord Ward, Earl of Dudley. Many of those present were disgruntled at the lack of any kind of progress but excited at the prospect that work might start again. Lord Ward told them what they wanted to hear:- *"Much time has been wasted in negotiations with other connecting companies and many hopes have been held out that these negotiations would have had a satisfactory issue. They have not done so however, and we have now met to place this undertaking on its proper footing as an independent line".*

The meeting went on to adopt a proposal by the Directors that a further £850,000 should be raised by the issuing of 6% preference shares. It was announced that two firms of well-established railway contractors had undertaken to complete the line within eighteen months. Messrs.Peto & Betts were to carry out the work north of Tipton and south of Worcester. Messrs.Treadwells would complete the middle section. Samuel Morton Peto and Edward Ledd Betts were building a reputation as railway contractors. Their partnership lasted from 1846 until 1872 and their works included the London Chatham & Dover Railway, the Grand Trunk Railway of Canada and a military railway in the Crimea which earned Peto a seat in the Lords as a baronet. Peto was a respectable chapel-going hard-working man with an apparent concern for his employees. He was also a 'control freak', with far more influence over the OWW than was reasonable. In this he was aided and abetted by his 'assistant', John Parson, a London solicitor of dubious reputation who became the railway's 'legal advisor'.

Peto and Parson were installed as directors and soon made their presence felt. The LNWR was completing its Bletchley-

Oxford line, which was denied access to the GWR's Oxford station, so the LNWR line approached the city alongside the Great Western for over a mile, terminating at Rewley Road. It opened in May 1851 and an Oxford-Bletchley-Euston service began. Parson and Peto had concluded an agreement earlier, on 21st February, with the LNWR and Midland railways, in which those companies would work the OWW - to be standard gauge only - for twenty years. They also wanted a line linking the OWW and LNWR near Oxford. The agreement had no weight in law and contravened the OWW Act regarding the gauge. Nevertheless, most shareholders voted in favour of this illegal arrangement, as did many of the Directors, puppets already in the hands of Parson and Peto. Lord Ward had no wish to be associated with any illegal activity so, referring to the Directors as 'a nonentity', he resigned after just one month in office.

First reaction came, not from the Great Western, but from its remaining supporters within the OWW, who brought legal action against their own company. The result, in May 1851, was an injunction restraining the OWW from carrying the agreement into effect. Most railways, that summer, were busy carrying unprecedented numbers of people, of all classes, up to London for the Great Exhibition at the Crystal Palace. The incomplete OWW meanwhile, endured a month of torment. On June 20th, utterly exceeding his brief and probably without batting an eyelid, Parson concluded an agreement for the working of the line - with the GWR! Parson no doubt thought he had events under control, but the shareholders meeting which was supposed to endorse the agreement refused to do so. After much discussion however, they did endorse it, subject to conditions. The GWR was to buy the OWW after four years, if required to do so, at a price of £30 for every £50 share. There was a note of desperation here as certain individuals tried to cut their losses. Each share was worth just £15 and falling - and John Parson was the largest individual shareholder. The Great Western promptly told Parson et al where they could put their shares, also warning that any attempt to build the line without broad gauge rails would be met with legal action. To add to the company's woes Francis Rufford went bankrupt on 26th June. The first Chairman had, despite all, remained a loyal supporter of the OWW, which had continued to have an account at Rufford & Wragge's Stourbridge bank. The £24,000 deposited there was lost. However, Moreton Peto, who obviously banked elsewhere, now offered financial support, so work was able to resume in earnest. Perhaps there was light at the end of the tunnel......

Reading the Riot Act

Campden Tunnel, sometimes known as Mickleton Tunnel, is half a mile long and situated four miles east of Honeybourne station. There is a rising gradient of 1:100 from Honeybourne, for 4½ miles, levelling out east of the tunnel on the approach to the site of Chipping Campden station. In 1851 the tunnel was still incomplete, thanks more to the personalities involved than difficulties with construction. In 1846 the tunnel contract had been awarded to Messrs.Ackroyd, Price and Williams. The first two departed after a dispute, leaving Williams to continue alone. In 1849 he was joined by a contractor named Marchant. Williams soon departed, at a time when work on the line had ceased. Work on the tunnel stopped in May, when Marchant, who claimed he was owed £4,300 by the OWW, felt unable to continue. Different accounts of the subsequent dispute and battle often contradict each other, so I have tried to unscramble them and give a description of events which is as near the truth as possible......

Work did not resume until 1851 by which time - foolishly or optimistically - Marchant had spent £10,000 on new plant. There was still no sign of the £4,300, so he soon halted work at the

tunnel. Parson and Peto were angered by this. Rather than negotiate, still less tackle the root cause of the problem by attempting to settle the disputed debt with Marchant, they persuaded some navvies to occupy the tunnel and seize all the plant. There was a violent skirmish between these men and a group loyal to Marchant, who beat off the invaders and retained possession of the tunnel. The situation was brought to Brunel's notice, although as he had had no opportunity to discuss it with Marchant, the account given to him must have been less than impartial. As Engineer, with work at long last in progress everywhere else along the route, a delay like this was unacceptable. Always a believer in the direct approach, on Friday 20th July 1851 he mustered a force of about 300 men and headed for the west end of the tunnel. Marchant had been forewarned and was waiting with about 100 men, armed with clubs, spades, etc. A magistrate was there and he succeeded in warning Brunel and his men off.

They returned the next day, Brunel having split his army into groups in order to mount a three-pronged assault on the tunnel defenders. He supposed that James Ashwin of Bretforton, the magistrate encountered the previous day, would have gone away. However, as his contingent approached the tunnel they found Ashwin, supported by other magistrates and a force of police armed with cutlasses. The magistrates had just read the Riot Act to Marchant's men and the police were disarming and dispersing them. Once the Riot Act had been read by a magistrate to a group of people rioting, or threatening to riot, they had to disperse within an hour or suffer the consequences. Ashwin then read the Riot Act to Brunel and his men, who were also disarmed. The Riot Act was read for a third time when Brunel's other two divisions blundered out of the woods shortly afterwards.

Marchant remained in control of the tunnel but the dispute was far from over. The magistrates did not return the next day, Sunday 22nd. Brunel used it to rally support, bringing in reinforcements from elsewhere on the OWW and the Birmingham & Oxford line. The B&O navvies were based at Warwick, about twenty miles to the north. They spent the latter part of the day travelling from their camp to the tunnel, no doubt disturbing the calm of the villages they passed through. What persuaded them - Brunel's force of character, the offer of a bonus, strong drink, the prospect of a good fight to relieve their humdrum lives? Whatever their motives, a large force of men was on the move. "Jackson's Oxford Journal", reported in its local news section for Chipping Norton (26th July) *"On Sunday night last our townspeople were surprised by the passing through of a band of 'navvies' on their way to the works of the (OWW) at Mickleton Hill, in 18 wagons, each containing about 25 occupants, who halted in the town for supper"*. They began to gather near the tunnel after midnight.

Marchant and about one hundred men were guarding the western end of the tunnel. Around 3am Brunel sent two hundred men forward. They reached the tunnel in some disorder, to be confronted in the darkness by Marchant, waving a pistol in each hand and threatening to shoot anyone who came closer. Brunel sent more men in and Marchant, leaving his force to continue as best they could, went for help. He returned about an hour later with magistrates, including James Ashwin, police and soldiers from the Gloucestershire Artillery. It seems likely that help was so close at hand because Ashwin had learnt of Brunel's plans, called on the forces of law and order and was, with them, already approaching the scene of the coming battle. (When starting his journey alone that night, Ashwin apparently had an almost surreal encounter with a group of Brunel's men, who asked him the way to the tunnel, so he took great satisfaction in misdirecting them to its east end.) Dawn was breaking, the opposing navvies could see

"Castle" Class No.7005 "Sir Edward Elgar" enters Chipping Campden tunnel with the 12.05pm Hereford-Paddington, 15th June 1963. It was a hot day, with window vents wide open and, according to custom, the front portion had been attached at Shrub Hill.

(Michael Mensing)

D7052, a 1,700hp diesel hydraulic 'Hymek', leaves Chipping Campden tunnel with the 5.25pm from Shrub Hill to Paddington, 18th June 1966.

(Michael Mensing)

each other properly for the first time, so fighting was able to begin in earnest. Men armed themselves with whatever weapons came to hand. The most vicious confrontations took place near the tunnel mouth. Within a short time most of Brunel's force was in the vicinity, an intimidating army many times the size of Marchant's.

So what did the heavily outnumbered forces of law and order do? It seems that the police and soldiers took little active part while the magistrates, as they were required to do, read the Riot Act. Few people could have heard it in the confusion and it had no effect. The magistrates then added a further bizarre dimension to the proceedings by advising Marchant to attempt to put his men to work! Alas, this was not a typical Monday morning, and their efforts were instantly thwarted by Brunel's men, who by now surrounded the whole site. There could easily have been a bloody climax at this point, with Brunel's men overwhelming Marchant's. Instead, skirmishing continued for several hours. Brunel himself, according to some reports, having earlier been sworn in by Ashwin as a special constable on the spot, toured the battlefield persuading his men not to kill the 'enemy'. Bruises, sore heads and broken limbs were numerous but no lives were lost. Marchant realised that his situation was hopeless and so, early in the afternoon, he personally 'surrendered' to Brunel. Extra troops had earlier been sent for. By the time they arrived from Coventry, at about 4 pm., their services were not required. "Jackson's Oxford Journal" said of the navvies, *On the following evening they returned with colours flying and hurrahing all through the town, evidently highly elated with the success of their mission*

Marchant lost everything except his honour. He held no personal grudge against Brunel, recognising that he was acting in the interests of the OWW. He knew where the blame really lay. In a letter to the "Railway Times" he commented, *I may leave Messrs.Peto & Betts to defend themselves against the charge of having consented to the march of over two thousand men on a Sunday for the purpose of taking possession of my property by force.*

Brunel's Influence

Brunel remained, first and foremost, Engineer of the Great Western Railway and champion of the broad gauge. He viewed the tactics of Parson and Peto with distaste. He was not dependent on the OWW for a living and felt increasingly at odds with the company because of its apparent antipathy to all things Great Western. He resigned on 17th March 1852, offering to help his successor, John Fowler, in any way that he could. Only four miles of the OWW had been opened before Brunel quit, but he left his mark on the whole route. The stations, track and viaducts were all unmistakably his.

The buildings at minor stations were adequate, simple, single-storey structures, wooden framed with clapboard walls, a tiled roof and canopy over the platform. Two small fireplaces, set at an angle in adjacent corners of the booking hall and waiting room, shared a tall chimney. Windows and doors were plain, like a doll's house. None of these buildings survives, although several - such as Fladbury, Ascott-under-Wychwood, Chipping Campden - lasted until the 1960s. More important intermediate stations had slightly larger buildings, still of the wooden chalet type, with round-arched windows and a hipped roof with awnings. Just one such building still exists on the OWW, at Charlbury.

Brunel's track was a 'baulk road', the baulks being longitudinal timbers directly under the rails, which were held in gauge by cross ties. It was awkward to lay and difficult to maintain, but gave a superb ride. Even after the broad gauge rail had been removed, the 'baulk road' continued on parts of the

OWW until at least the 1880s. The long intervals between the cross ties could prove useful in absorbing energy when there was a derailment; the absence of sleepers often helped derailed vehicles to stay upright. A northbound express was passing through Hartlebury one evening in 1854 when the locomotive, No.14, shed a tyre from a rear driving wheel but - the diary of David Joy, Locomotive Superintendent of the OWW, noted - *it held in one big open ring on the engine, till she stuck in the longitudinal timbers, stopping all quietly, almost without shaking the passengers*. The engine in question was a new 2-4-0, built by Hawthorns in 1853, given the GW number 178 ten years later and scrapped as late as 1902.

When the GWR spread into Devon and Cornwall the many valleys which lay in the path of the railway were crossed by spectacular Brunel-designed timber viaducts. There were six such viaducts on the OWW, five of them north of Worcester - at Evesham, Hoobrook, Blakedown, Stambermill, Brettell Lane and Parkhead. The vertical timbers of these viaducts were grouped in sets of five, cross braced with horizontal and diagonal members to form every 'pillar', with a deck above. Springing from each 'pillar' five sets of five timbers splayed out, like fingers, supporting an upper deck which carried the track. The large timber railway viaduct was a new concept, devised by Brunel, cheap to construct and easy to maintain because individual timbers were of standardised lengths. They could be replaced as required, often without interrupting traffic - these structures were almost prefabricated. The wood was usually Baltic pine, proofed against decay and fire by a process known as kyanising (after its inventor, J.H.Kyan). When the OWW was built good quality Baltic pine was plentiful and easily affordable but within thirty years it became scarce and prohibitively expensive. No other wood was as suitable, durable and cheap, so the viaducts became uneconomic. Surprisingly, two on the OWW were not demolished but 'preserved'. Brettell Lane, which was 390 feet long with a maximum height of 55 feet, was filled in and an embankment built around it, consisting partly of rubble and waste materials from foundries in the area. Parkhead, a 490 foot long viaduct spanning the canal at Blower's Green, was encased in brick in the second half of 1877 - *A contract to supply 1,000,000 of the latter has been secured by Messrs.Phillips and McEwan of Dudley* ('Brierley Hill Advertiser'). Stambermill was, apparently, a cause of worry for people living in its shadow - and with a height of 100 feet and a length of almost 600 feet the shadow was substantial. As early as 1871 they wanted it 'filled in'. There were several minor accidents in its vicinity. More serious was a mishap on 15th October 1876, when a southbound train of parcels vans had split at Brettell Lane. The footplate crew continued unawares, slowing as usual on the approach to Stambermill. The detached vans caught up, collided with the rest of the train and pushed several vehicles over the side of the viaduct. There were no injuries but nearby residents understandably renewed their pleas for it to be filled in. Instead, a replacement was built alongside, a ten-arched viaduct of four million blue bricks, erected in less than four months (20th September 1881-11th January 1882) at a cost of £13,835. At the same time and in the same manner the contractors, Kellett & Bentley, were replacing Blakedown. Hoobrook, south of Kidderminster, was the largest viaduct. A twenty-arched replacement was built during 1884-85. The Evesham viaduct over the Avon had been replaced some ten years earlier. Most minor bridges north of Evesham, seventy-one altogether according to one source, were also made of wood, but they too went the way of the viaducts. Most bridges east of Evesham - and the facings of Campden Tunnel - were of local stone, from the quarry at Taynton, south of Shipton-under-Wychwood.

A posed photograph at Adlestrop, as the crowded footplate of a 'Dean Goods' drifts towards Oxford - broad gauge goods shed, OWW platform building, immaculate gardens, standard issue GWR stationmaster's house. About 1920.

(Oxfordshire County Council Photographic Archive)

Evesham station with OWW buildings, from a photograph taken about 1880 which appeared in "Railway Magazine" in 1907. There is a broad gauge goods shed, a dip in the platform for the barrow crossing and one track is still laid as a baulk road. The footbridge is a Great Western addition.

(author's collection)

Brunel's viaduct at Stambermill, about 1865.   *(courtesy of Stourbridge Library, Dudley Library Services)*

Old and new viaducts at Hoobrook, Kidderminster, looking south.   *(Museum Service, Wyre Forest District Council)*

The second Hoobrook Viaduct, about 1890, with a northbound train crossing. The area is much altered, although most cottages still stand; not so the paper mill, seen through the arches. Until it was developed in 1976, the land in the foreground was ideal for toboggan races in the winter.

(Museum Service, Wyre Forest District Council)

37 040 and 37 077 cross Parkhead Viaduct with train 6V69 Bescot-Cardiff, 10th March 1993, nine days before the line closed north of Round Oak. The condition of this viaduct, built around Brunel's original wooden structure, was giving cause for concern.

(Paul Dorney; Ned Williams collection)

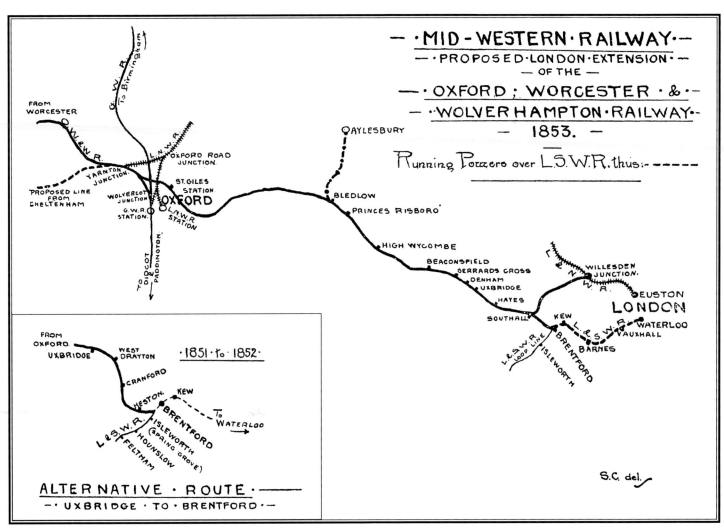

The OWW at its most fanciful, the 1853 scheme for an independent line to London, which would have had access to Euston and Waterloo. Illustrated in the "Railway Magazine", 1907.

(author's collection)

The London Extension

At the beginning of 1852 work was virtually complete between Evesham and Stourbridge. Before trains could run three major difficulties had to be overcome. First, funds were almost exhausted. Second, there was no rolling stock and nobody with the expertise to buy any.

Third, Parson and Peto were diverting attention from these urgent matters by continuing to promote a scheme for the extension of the OWW as an independent main line to London. They did not, of course, explain how such a thing could ever be financed. Plans for an Oxford & Brentford line (also called the Mid-Western scheme) were drawn up late in 1850. It was to leave the OWW north of Oxford, with a station on the edge of the city at St.Giles, running via High Wycombe and Southall to Brentford, where it would join the London & South Western Railway and have running rights into Waterloo. The prospect of this line, creaming off some of their traffic, antagonised both the GWR and LNWR. The Bill was rejected by the Commons in just fifteen days in the 1851 session. A virtually identical Bill received similar treatment the following year. 1853 saw a modified Bill, with the addition of a line from Southall to Willesden Junction, giving the Mid-Western/OWW access to both Waterloo and Euston! There was also provision for what would have been an important cross-country line, leaving the OWW at Yarnton to go via Witney and Burford to Cheltenham.

In the same session the LNWR presented a Bill reviving plans for a Tring-Oxford line. The Mid-Western scheme was rejected by the Commons; the Tring line by the Lords. However, a Bill for a short double track link between Yarnton and the LNWR's Oxford-Bletchley line - the so-called Buckinghamshire Junction Railway, usually known as the 'Yarnton Loop' - was passed into law. When it opened on 1st April 1854, OWW expresses used it to run to Euston via Bletchley although, as the "History of the London & North Western Railway" (pub.1914) acknowledged, *"it must be confessed that the journey was somewhat of the roundabout order"*. Handborough assumed an importance out of all proportion to its size, with extra sidings, a refreshment room and a new nameboard inscribed 'Handborough Junction'. There were four OWW trains a day to/from Euston. When a southbound train arrived at Handborough an LNW locomotive took over from the OWW one. Three carriages were normally detached from the rear before the main train continued to Bletchley, where it was attached to a Euston express. Once the main train had cleared the junction, at Yarnton, the OWW engine which had brought it from Worcester took its three remaining carriages to Oxford GWR station. Here, despite the poor relations between the OWW and GWR, there were good connections to Paddington. A similar pattern operated in reverse. The service continued until September 1861.

A down stopping train, hauled by a Dean 4-4-0, leaves Handborough, about 1900.

(Stephen Widdowson collection)

David Joy

Meanwhile, early in 1852, main line services had not yet begun, there was no rolling stock of any kind. When the "Worcestershire Chronicle & Provincial Railway Gazette" announced on March 10th that a few days earlier a locomotive had traversed the line *"from within a quarter of a mile of Evesham to within a quarter of a mile of Stourbridge"*, it was either a rumour or a contractor's engine. The opening date for the core Evesham-Stourbridge section, 1st May, loomed ever larger. The Directors had no clear idea what to do and it was left to John Fowler, Brunel's successor and a thoroughly professional railwayman, to suggest a way out. He advised that the line be worked under contract by C.C.Williams, a London carriage builder. Williams accepted, his first task being to appoint a Locomotive Superintendent. He 'networked' colleagues in the rail industry, including E.B.Wilson, owner of the Railway Foundry at Leeds, who suggested David Joy. Wilson had appointed him manager of the drawing office at Leeds in 1844, aged just 19. He had soon gained a reputation designing locos with a 2-2-2 wheel arrangement, the 'Jenny Lind' type (named after the Swedish opera singer, 1820-87). In 1850 Joy had been made Locomotive Superintendent of the Nottingham & Grantham Railway, a line ready to open but with no engines. He obtained some and, against the odds, the railway opened on time. This experience was to stand him in good stead on the OWW. Early in 1852, living in Leeds and temporarily unemployed, he called in at the Railway Foundry, where he heard about the OWW and asked his former boss for advice or, as his diary records, *"Got big geological map, and spotted it out, very sanguine to get into such a nice neighbourhood. Saw E.B.Wilson and worked up for it."*

The pace of life in the nineteenth century could be surprisingly swift, due in no small measure to an efficient postal service and the growing railway system. A few weeks after his visit to the Foundry, Joy received a letter from Wilson, written earlier the same day, *"telling me to meet him at C.C.William's office next morning at 10am in London. I was off like a shot that afternoon at 4 o'clock by Great Northern Railway"*. The interview took place, on April 19th, and Joy was appointed with immediate effect. It was now a race against time. The words of Joy's own diary, extracts from which were published in "Railway Magazine" in 1907-08, suggest the frantic nature of his life during the next few days - *"Went to Welwyn - and got "Mudlark", a contractor's engine, to Offord - got a big six-coupled long boiler, by Stephenson, in very good condition. Then next day to Shrewsbury to hire Shrewsbury & Hereford engines; had to see Jeffrey before breakfast, but he could spare none. On to Leeds and Pontefract after a four-coupled "Jenny", a contractor's engine, just put in fine order at Railway Foundry, with the cheque (£1,250) in my pocket to pay for it. Then to Leeds to see a little engine in the shops at Railway Foundry - called "Canary"; she was a little mite. Arranged for all these to go to Worcester"*. These locos were lettered by the OWW, rather than numbered. 'A' was the 'Jenny', 'B' the long boiler and named "Jack of Newbury", "Canary" was 'C', "Mudlark" was 'F'. The OWW opened on Saturday 1st May 1852 with these four engines to serve all the needs of 36 miles of main line railway. Reinforcements, locos 'D' and 'E' - long-boiler types borrowed from the North Staffordshire Railway - arrived at Worcester by 7th May. This was just the beginning ....

[Diary : Feastings and Openings : Broad Gauge Special :
Old Worse & Worse? : Round Oak : Expansion and Absorption]

Diary

1852
1st May : Special train between Stourbridge and Evesham. Normal service two days later.

July : Double track now in use between Norton Junction and Evesham. Fifty-two acres of land bought by OWW at Shrub Hill for £8,500, for locomotive, carriage and wagon works.

20th December : OWW opened to passengers, Stourbridge-Dudley (opened to goods on 16th November). Stations at Brettell Lane, Brierley Hill & Round Oak, Netherton, Dudley.

1853
4th June : Oxford-Evesham opened.

4th August : Act granting running powers to GWR over OWW, Priestfield-Cannock Road Junction, also to OWW over GWR, Wolvercot Junction-Oxford.

1st December : Dudley-Tipton opened, including a link to the LNWR Stour Valley Line at Tipton, the first Tipton Curve. (Another, unrelated Tipton Curve, completing the triangular junction of the Princes End branch with the Stour Valley line, opened in 1883.)

1854
18th March : Evesham-Honeybourne up line closed because it was standard gauge only, contrary to the terms of the Act. Re-opening permitted on 20th March 1855, after a broad gauge up rail had been laid and the line doubled to Campden. Mixed gauge double track earlier brought into use, Charlbury-Handborough, 1st August 1854. The twenty miles between Charlbury and Campden remained mixed gauge single track until August 1858, when it became double track - standard gauge only.

1st April : OWW began a service between Wolverhampton and London Euston.

13th April : Broad gauge train travelled the whole line, Oxford to Wolverhampton.

1st July : Final part of OWW main line opened to passengers, Tipton-Cannock Road Junction. Stations at Daisey Bank, Bilston, Priestfield and Wolverhampton. (The line had opened to goods in April; the spelling of Daisy Bank was corrected in February 1866.)

14th November : Mixed gauge GWR line opened, Birmingham Snow Hill-Wolverhampton, joining the OWW at Priestfield. Mixed gauge link opened, Cannock Road-Stafford Road junctions, Victoria Basin goods branch converted from standard to mixed gauge.

1856
20th December : Princes End station opened.

1857
20th July : Round Oak & Brierley Hill renamed Round Oak.

1858
23rd August : Round Oak accident. (The date was incorrectly given as 23rd April in my earlier book, "Rails Through The Hills".)

December : Brierley Hill station opened.

1860
14th June : OWW amalgamated with the Worcester & Hereford, and Newport Abergavenny & Hereford, to form the West Midland Railway, with effect from 1st July 1860.

1861
1st July : OWW section of West Midland Railway managed by a Joint Committee, WM and GWR (prior to final GWR absorption in 1863).

1st October : Through service Wolverhampton-Worcester-Paddington commenced; Wolverhampton-Worcester-Euston trains ceased the previous day.

1862
The opening date of Hagley station is uncertain, but it first appeared in time tables this year.

1863
1st August : West Midland Railway absorbed by GWR, as empowered by an Act of 13th July.

Feastings and Openings

When the line opened between Evesham and Stourbridge in 1852 it was standard gauge, single track from Evesham to Norton Junction (doubled two months later), then double to Stourbridge. Extra baulks were provided to carry the broad gauge rails, which were yet to be laid. The only train on 1st May was a special. Those on board - the Directors, John Fowler, Williams, Parson, Peto, Joy, etc. - were about to experience a day of self-congratulation and overindulgence. The train left Stourbridge, pulled by engine 'A', at 9am, accompanied by cheers from the crowds, cannon fire and the peeling of church bells. Greeted all along the route, it passed through several triumphal floral arches and arrived at Evesham just before noon, where an estimated ten thousand people had gathered. Those aboard walked to the Town Hall for a lunch provided by the Mayor and Corporation. There were speeches of course, during which Morton Peto reminded everyone of his own agenda, the London extension, which *"should and must be made"*. At 2pm the train left Evesham, after which about 700 working men sat down to a meal at long rows of trestle tables laid out in the High Street. After they had finished, it was the women's turn to be feasted. The weather was fine and, it being May Day, there was plenty of street theatre, with acrobats, mummers, etc.

When the special arrived at Shrub Hill, its well-fed passengers were offered cake and wine by the Mayor of Worcester. After this it continued to Kidderminster - for a celebratory banquet! This was held at the Lion Hotel, in the town centre and down the hill from the station (Woolworths now occupies the site). There were more speeches and more enthusiasm for the London extension. Lord Ward, Earl of Dudley, according to the supplement in the "Illustrated London News" (8th May 1852), claimed that *"without this measure it is impossible to hope that the great mineral and other resources of the western counties could ever be adequately developed"*. At about 7pm some directors needed to return to Droitwich to catch a Midland connecting train. The driver of the special had gone missing so

Evesham station on opening day, as featured in the "Illustrated London News", complete with Brunel buildings, open trucks, basic signalling and England flag.   *(author's collection)*

Feasting at Evesham, 1st May 1852, from the "Illustrated London News", 8th May 1852.   *(author's collection)*

Joy *"took the engine myself and did splendidly till I had delivered my passengers to Droitwich. Then in running back round my carriages the station master himself turned the wrong points and shot me off the road on the bridge over the canal - tender first. Somehow I had not a thought of my own personal danger .... My only idea was my engine, - she was badly off the road .... so I at once got hold of the contractor's engine "Jack of Newbury" .... and got to Kidderminster as fast as I could to fetch my directors, etc. Utterly done up, I got to Worcester, and to bed"*. He spent the next day helping to re-rail 'A', adding, *"she was no worse. We opened the line on the Monday with nothing to remember - just these four engines.*

The mishap at Droitwich was one of many, but Joy thrived on a challenge. One Sunday in 1852 his diary noted, *"I was fetched out of chapel, an engine off the road at Campden. Took old 'B' and spent the day there; but it was a lovely day, so we enjoyed it"*.

He also kept an account of the working costs of the OWW. For the first three months, May-July 1852, the six locos consumed 355 tons of coke at a cost of £332. To encourage efficient and economical driving, Joy began awarding a 'coke premium' of £10 and £5 every six months to the two train crews who used the least amount of fuel. He reasoned that, *"if a driver worked his engine so as to save coke it meant his looking after her in every way ... so the engine at the top of the coke list mostly was the best in condition"*. The wages bill for May-July 1852 was £335 and salaried staff accounted for £69 (all figures rounded to the nearest £). Total expenses amounted to £859. One item, "Midland Railway locomotive power - £6", could mean that Midland engine(s) had been hired at a busy period. Difficulties were made worse by unfinished facilities, prompting Joy to note, *"Of course we began without shops or tools, and a most shabby shed at Worcester, for two engines. I could only get repairs at a little smith's place which had a lathe that could turn a valve spindle. Meanwhile I did my own valve settings"*. A properly equipped workshop was eventually ready for use by March 1855.

The problems of operating a main line railway with just six locos, all different from each other, no spare parts and a repair shop without tools, can easily be imagined. At the beginning there were four trains in each direction between Stourbridge and Evesham, taking just under two hours, with two short workings between Stourbridge and Kidderminster. There were two Sunday trains, morning and evening, with an early afternoon short working between Stourbridge and Worcester. Unusually for the time, all trains carried first, second and third class passengers. The first time-tables showed stations at Evesham, Fladbury, Pershore, Worcester, Fearnall Heath (sic), Droitwich, Hartlebury, Kidderminster and Stourbridge.

Meanwhile, the Droitwich-Stoke Works Junction section, a double track standard gauge OWW line, had opened a little before the festivities at Evesham and Kidderminster, on 18th February 1852. It completed the Worcester Loop and all Midland Railway expresses used it from the beginning. A connecting service was introduced on the old main line but, unsurprisingly, it was little used. It withered until just one daily train in each direction called at Spetchley, Dunhampstead and Droitwich Road before those stations closed to passengers at the end of September 1855. Just on the northern end of the loop there was a station at Stoke Works. It replaced the earlier station of the same name, which was on the old main line. Although an OWW station it was served only by Midland Railway trains. This was strange but logical, as the Midland could offer it a limited service 'in passing', whereas the OWW could not, as its trains had no right of access to the Midland's tracks, which began at the junction a

few yards to the north. The station and adjacent goods branches, both OWW and Midland, served the salt works, founded in 1828 and acquired in 1852 by John Corbett. He went on to become the local MP and Droitwich's 'salt king', had the Chateau Impney built as his home and, near the end of his life, part-financed the modernisation of Droitwich station in 1899. An account of Stoke Works station ("Railway Magazine" July 1953) also records that the track layout at Droitwich was not as originally intended. There would have been direct access only between Hartlebury and Stoke Works, so direct running on the Worcester Loop would not have been possible. This was corrected by an amendment, in the Act of 3rd August 1846, providing for a "Droitwich Junction Line" just under half a mile long. The original line was also built, completing a triangle north of Droitwich station, but it was never more than a little used freight spur, converted into sidings about 1890.

Two other curiosities persisted on the Worcester Loop for many years. Some Midland Railway expresses called at both Worcester and Droitwich but passengers travelling between them were not allowed to use such trains; they were local passengers and had to use the trains of the local company, the OWW. Similarly the OWW station near the southern end of the loop was Norton Junction but, for passengers using it, the junction did not exist. Only Worcester-Oxford local trains called. Over the years a Worcester-Gloucester local service developed, with a local station south of Norton at Wadborough. All these trains passed Norton without stopping, an anomaly which persisted until closure in the 1960s.

In July 1852 the OWW paid £8,500 for 52 acres of land west of Shrub Hill station, where the locomotive, carriage and wagon works would be erected. In addition, the six mile section between Stourbridge and Dudley had opened by the end of the year, to goods on 16th November and to passengers on 20th December. There were new stations at Brettell Lane, Round Oak (named 'Brierley Hill & Round Oak' at first), Netherton and Dudley. At first the line was single track north of Brettell Lane.

An order was placed with R.W.Hawthorn of Newcastle for twenty locomotives, eleven 2-4-0 passenger types and nine 0-6-0s for freight. Five passenger and six freight locos had arrived by the end of 1852. These locos were all delivered to Worcester, which had two engine sheds north of Shrub Hill. There was a four-road terminal shed for goods locos, and a three-road through shed for passenger engines, on a curve. They were a familiar part of the railway landscape from 1852 until demolition in 1969 (goods) and 1989 (passenger).

The new locomotives were the first on the OWW to be fitted with a weatherboard, a metal shield at the front of the footplate, pierced with two circular windows. It would be many years before proper cabs were provided for the crew. David Joy wasted no time in experiencing - and logging - a ride on the footplate of newly delivered 2-4-0 No.1 "Hawthorn". Weatherboard or no, the wind chill must have been real enough as this 30 ton engine, with a featherweight service train of three carriages and a van, took 8 minutes 55 seconds from Kidderminster almost to Stourbridge, where a signal check slowed it to 4mph. The train averaged 53mph, with a top speed of 64mph near Blakedown. Today's non-stop dmus are booked to take 11 minutes.

Joy was on the footplate again, probably in November 1854, when someone appeared unannounced, wanting to play trains - *"Sometimes our big people cared to see how it was done. One dark, stormy night our chairman, Lord Redesdale, stepped onto the footplate at Charlbury .... and he said he should like to see 60 miles per hour. It was the night up express, J.Burt and No.17 this time. "Certainly, your lordship" said I, and told Joe....I gave his*

A wartime view of Worcester, with a wide variety of locomotive types and both OWW sheds in frame. *(Jim Peden collection)*

Worcester OWW passenger engine shed, with "Castle" No.7011, 8th September 1963. The shed closed to steam in December 1965.

(C.A.Appleton, Jim Peden collection)

lordship my usual stand at the left weather-board. He wore an ordinary overcoat and a top hat. After about a mile run, he leaned over to me to ask if this was 60 miles. "Not yet, but soon", I said. In another half mile his lordship was grasping the handrail with the left and his hat with his right, like grim death - we were on it, rushing like mad a little over 60 miles per hour - not much to us but with his "rig-out" I don't think he liked it. I knew it was not nice, but he could not say stay, he had too much pluck; and he had to "grin and bide it" for five more miles"

Following the opening between Evesham and Stourbridge in May 1852, there had been a steady improvement as new locomotives were delivered, men were encouraged to operate them efficiently and - belatedly - plans were made to equip repair shops and build workshops. The OWW was at last earning a living, coaxed along by three professional railwaymen, C.C.Williams, contracted to operate the line, John Fowler and David Joy.

By the spring of 1853 the section between Evesham and Wolvercot Junction was almost ready to open. Parson and Peto had always wanted the whole line to be mixed gauge, so as to further links with the LNWR and to pursue their dreams of an independent line to London. The Great Western had argued that, under the terms of the 1845 Act, the OWW should be broad gauge only between Abbotswood and Wolvercot junctions. This expectation, at a time when the broad gauge was so obviously doomed, was as unrealistic as Parson's dream of a London line. Common sense intervened in March 1853, when the Law Courts dismissed a Great Western appeal and confirmed an earlier judgment of 1852. This ruled that although the OWW was required to be *"formed of such a gauge .... as will admit of the same being worked continuously with the said Great Western Railway"*, this did not prevent it from laying down additional rails of a different gauge. The Great Western could hardly complain, as its Oxford & Rugby line, which linked Oxford with the start of the OWW proper at Wolvercot Junction, was mixed gauge anyway, so no extra expense or sacrifice of principle was involved. As the OWW had no broad gauge rolling stock, the Great Western knew that any OWW trains admitted onto its lines would be standard gauge. However, the GWR remained on high alert as a matter of principle, threatening legal action whenever the OWW seemed inclined to 'forget' about providing broad gauge rails over any part of its line.

The permanent way between Wolvercot Junction and Evesham was nearing completion as a mixed gauge single track, on the down line, with passing places. The opening date was fixed as 21st April 1853, postponed until 7th May after some earth movements near the western end of Campden Tunnel. There was a serious slip at the tunnel mouth, so the trackbed was packed from underneath with longitudinal timbers, in several layers, giving it the appearance of a small trestle bridge and the nickname 'Birdcage'. Trains had to be hand signalled over it. Captain Galton, on behalf of the Board of Trade, inspected the line in this condition, but refused to sanction opening, as the broad gauge rails, and the junction at Wolvercot, were incomplete. The OWW Directors decided to run the planned special on 7th May anyway. A double-headed train, with twenty-six coaches of invited guests, left Dudley early in the morning, calling at all stations en route, with a champagne lunch provided at Evesham. Pomp gave way to farce at Wolvercot when everyone detrained, walking across the unfinished junction to board a Great Western train to Oxford. Here there was a banquet with the traditional speeches, at which Peto made his own traditional references to the London extension. At least one speaker had something new to say, when remarking how the university authorities' hostility to the Great Western 'branch',

opened nine years earlier, had evaporated as they had come to realise that *"the interests of Oxford could only be promoted by keeping pace with the rest of the world"*. There was tragedy on the return journey near the 'Birdcage', David Joy on the footplate, *"the line all covered and guarded by navvies and platelayers. Returning late at night, with every point signalled I was on the leading engine, and both were running tender first. The light at the end of the tunnel where the slip was, did not appear, so we slackened down, and passed the slip very slowly, seeing nothing of the light or man. Next morning we were told we had gone over him.*

Galton inspected the line a second time on 14th May, but the broad gauge track remained incomplete and the OWW and GWR signals and points at Wolvercot could not be made to operate in conjunction with each other. Galton called again on 28th May, but refused to carry out an inspection when John Fowler told him that much of the broad gauge rail would not bear the weight of a train. There followed four days of feverish activity, during which permanent way gangs worked round the clock to render it usable. On the morning of Thursday 2nd June 1853, Captain Sir Douglas Strutt Galton carried out his fourth inspection, this time with a broad gauge train hired from the GWR, travelling from Wolvercot to Evesham without incident. Until the second track was laid, his report stated that the line could open but must be worked in two sections, either side of Charlbury, with a pilotman accompanying each train through each section. The facing points were to be passed at very slow speed. Trains began running on 4th June. There were nine new stations, at Handborough, Charlbury, Ascott-under-Wychwood, Shipton, Adlestrop, Moreton-in-Marsh, Blockley, Campden and Honeybourne. There were five trains a day between Oxford and Dudley, only two of which called at all stations and carried third class passengers. There were some short workings north of Kidderminster. Sundays saw two through trains, with no fewer than eight short workings between Dudley and Kidderminster, all with third class.

Most of the route was now open but once again events off the line would interfere with the smooth running of the railway itself. This was a time of international tension, with the onset of the Crimean War, causing the OWW Chairman, Captain Rushout, to spend most of his time with his regiment at Aldershot. Routine management was left in the hands of the new Deputy Chairman - John Parson. By September 1853 he had concluded the agreement to route the line's London traffic via the LNWR to Euston. The Euston service began the following April, on completion of the 'Yarnton Loop' link line but prior to that, on 1st December 1853, opening of the OWW between Dudley and Tipton meant trains could continue to Wolverhampton (High Level) via a link with the LNWR, the so-called Tipton Curve. So far as Parson was concerned, the Great Western and its broad gauge were becoming irrelevant.

This impression was reinforced further when the track was doubled between Evesham and Wolvercot. Trains no longer had to pass at a station loop, so the service could be improved. The new up line was standard gauge only and there were no plans to provide a broad gauge rail. The Railways Department at the Board of Trade was not made aware that the track had been doubled, but an official noticed that trains were due to pass between Evesham and Honeybourne, on what was supposed to be a single line. Enquiries were met by a rebuff from Parson, who said that passenger trains towards Oxford were running on a new standard gauge track. He continued by claiming that Captain Galton's earlier refusal to sanction the opening *"for the reasons he gave was not within his functions"*. All parties knew that the OWW was supposed to be broad gauge; they also knew the broad gauge was doomed. However, Parson's confrontational attitude

A locomotive with weatherboard, almost certainly ex-OWW, poses for the camera at Honeybourne, about 1885. The camera is facing Oxford and the Great Western buildings have replaced the OWW originals. In yellow brick with red courses, the design is standard for the time and similar to buildings which used to stand on the Worcester platform at Kidderminster, erected in 1877. When today's railwaymen talk of bi-directional signalling, this is not what they mean! *(Jim Clemens collection)*

at this point probably prevented a common-sense solution. Instead, the Board of Trade felt obliged to meet his challenge with one of their own, so in March 1854 they obtained an injunction banning use of the new track until a broad gauge rail was laid. Trains reverted to using the single mixed gauge line. There followed a stubborn ritual as, every month, Captain Galton inspected the new line, always refusing to let it open because it remained standard gauge only. After bombarding the Board with a series of appeals, to no avail, Parson realised that he would have to do something totally out of character - submit. The broad gauge was laid on the second line, which reopened in March 1855.

Meanwhile, on the approach to Wolverhampton, the OWW was met at Priestfield by the GWR mixed gauge main line from Birmingham Snow Hill, not yet completed. The Wolverhampton station was east of the town centre, adjacent to the LNWR station, which was on higher ground. This 'Low Level' was a joint station, shared between the OWW, GWR and the Shrewsbury & Birmingham, a small independent company that was a pawn in the power struggle between the LNWR and Great Western. OWW mixed gauge tracks, over which the GWR had

running rights, continued beyond Low Level to Cannock Road Junction. This was where the GWR line to Shrewsbury curved to the west, and an OWW standard gauge link with the Grand Junction line continued towards Bushbury. The OWW had briefly considered not building the Tipton-Priestfield-Wolverhampton-Bushbury Junction section, content to run all its trains via the Tipton Curve into the LNWR High Level station. But the GWR, with its nominally independent client, the Birmingham Wolverhampton & Dudley Railway, wanted this link for access to Low Level and beyond, so applied to Parliament for powers to build it themselves. By the time they did so however, the OWW had decided that construction would go ahead and work had already begun at Tipton. A Parliamentary Select Committee examined the GWR application and rejected it. Matters were resolved by the Act of August 4th 1853, in which the GWR obtained running powers over OWW tracks north of Priestfield and in return the OWW was given running powers over the GWR into Oxford. So, loose ends were tied up at both ends - literally - and, much to the surprise of many, the OWW found itself with a mixed gauge line throughout.

Broad Gauge Special

Broad gauge rails were not always provided for both lines of double track, but the broad gauge was uninterrupted and capable of carrying a train. E.T.MacDermot, in his "History of the Great Western Railway" (1931) wrote, *"The only recorded instance of a broad-gauge train running over any part of the line south of Priestfield was Captain Galton's inspection trip from Wolvercot to Evesham and back on 2nd June 1853. There was a legend .... that a broad gauge engine once penetrated as far as Dudley, but this can only be accepted with great doubt. It is most unlikely that the broad-gauge rail beyond Evesham was ever in a state to carry an engine.* Subsequent books and articles about the OWW have repeated this assertion, including my own "Rails Through The Hills". However, Michael Hale, of Dudley, has produced evidence to show that MacDermot was wrong. This from "The Times" of Monday 17th April 1854 - *"Oxford Worcester & Wolverhampton Railway - On Thursday a broad gauge train travelled along this line the whole length from Oxford to Wolverhampton to prove the capability of using the extra rail. A party of the directors accompanied the train".*

It appears that a number of people who travelled on the train recorded their impressions in sworn affidavits, set down to support either the OWW contention that its broad gauge was fit to use, or the Great Western claim that it was only a token gesture. Using documents lodged at the BRB Records Centre, and at the Public Record Office, Michael Hale painstakingly assembled an account of what happened that day. He describes it in "Brunel's Broad Gauge in the Black Country", published in 1997, and I am grateful for his permission to relate the main events here.

On 11th April the OWW company secretary wrote to his GWR counterpart requesting the use of a broad gauge engine and carriage for the purpose of journeying over the down line from Oxford to Wolverhampton. The request was granted and the special, hauled by a Gooch-designed 2-2-2 Jenny Lind named "Arrow", consisted of one first and one second class carriage. John Fowler, with John Whitton, resident engineer, travelled on the 9.15 service train from Paddington to Oxford. No less a person than Brunel was waiting on the platform, determined to travel on the footplate of the special to 'inspect the line', even adding that he would not permit the train to run without him. His attitude seemed quite insensitive of the fact that he was no longer OWW Engineer; neither was he prepared to trust the judgment of the man who was. On the other hand, perhaps no offence to Fowler was intended; as father of the broad gauge, it seemed to him only natural that he should be allowed to ride the footplate on this important new line. Maybe Fowler too, had been 'advised' not to let any important member of the GWR onto the train; although it belonged to the GWR the OWW intended to instal their own driver and fireman for the run to Wolverhampton. In any event, there was a frank exchange of views between the two men and Fowler refused to let Brunel travel, either on the footplate or on board the train. Brunel telegraphed Paddington for instructions. After receiving them he reluctantly agreed that the train could run without him, but insisted that William Wright, one of the GWR's most experienced drivers, should be at the controls. The intended OWW driver, Thomas Davison, acted as fireman. Fowler, Whitton and Frederick Hayward, who I shall refer to later, also squeezed onto the footplate. The train left Oxford at 11.30, stopping at Evesham for water and at Worcester for a leisurely meal. A set of steps on the second class carriage was bent and slightly out of gauge, causing the train to pass

through all stations at low speed, striking the ironwork of a bridge at Fladbury and damaging a water pipe at Dudley, although the various affidavits could not agree on this. The double track mixed gauge line north of Tipton had been inspected by Captain H.W.Tyler only the previous day. He noted that Wolverhampton station was incomplete - the platforms were unfinished, there were no platform buildings, no sidings, no working signals. The special steamed into this barren landscape at 6.30pm. Whitton later claimed that Wright told him the track was in excellent condition and he would not hesitate to bring a broad gauge train up from Oxford in two hours if the line were kept clear of other traffic.

The train had to return to Oxford, but there was as yet no working turntable or crossover at Wolverhampton, so "Arrow" ran tender first, propelling the carriages. It was now running in the up direction on the down line, preceded by a standard gauge pilot engine on the up line. When the special arrived at a station, the pilot continued to the next station, where instructions were given that no down train should set out until the special had cleared the section. Progress was very slow and, for the driver, very uncomfortable. Wright had to drive as far as Evesham, site of the 'first' broad gauge crossover, in a very precarious position indeed - one foot on the hand rail, the other on the quadrant housing the reversing lever and one hand on the regulator. Only in this manner could he drive the train and see the line ahead over the carriage roofs in the gathering darkness. As Michael Hale commented, "He would have been very pleased to arrive at Evesham". (Whitton later admitted that he had overlooked a broad gauge crossover at Bilston.) The train continued from Evesham, locomotive at the head now, still wrong road but without a pilot - the only down train, a night goods, was held at Handborough - reaching Oxford at 5am the following morning, Good Friday.

I failed to find a mention of the broad gauge special in the local press, although did notice that the "Worcester Herald" (15th April 1854) featured front page advertisements for dating agencies! - *"This Institution has been established for many years (with great success) as a medium for the introduction of parties unknown to each other who are desirous of forming Matrimonial Alliances...."*, while another announced more plainly, *"Matrimony Made Easy, or How To Win A Lover"*.

The final part of the OWW main line, north of Tipton, opened to normal traffic on 1st July, with stations at Daisey Bank, Bilston, Priestfield and Wolverhampton. The "Wolverhampton Chronicle" (5th July 1854) reported that the first train left at 8am, without ceremony. Some trains continued to be routed over the LNWR route north of Tipton for a while, probably because the Low Level station still resembled a building site, so the paper cautioned its readers that, *"as many (trains) run from the high level station, a little consultation of the time-tables will be necessary"*. The OWW now had a service from Wolverhampton of 10 trains a day to Kidderminster, 7 to Worcester, 5 to Evesham and 4 to Oxford and London (Euston). The Great Western line from Birmingham Snow Hill opened on 14th November, joining the OWW at Priestfield. Paddington-Birmingham-Wolverhampton expresses briefly ran on the broad gauge, until September 1861, and local broad gauge services from Birmingham ceased in October 1868. When travelling between Priestfield and Wolverhampton these Great Western services were the only regular broad gauge trains ever to run on the OWW.

6828 "Trellech Grange" arrives at Priestfield with the 4.48pm Wolverhampton-Worcester stopping train, 1st June 1957. The main line to Birmingham curves sharply to the right. As at Stourbridge, the OWW was the first line to be built and so had the better alignment at the junction.   *(Roger Carpenter collection)*

Next to Brunel, the champion of the broad gauge was Daniel Gooch, Chief Mechanical Engineer of the GWR, 1837-1864. On 18th January 1953 "Castle" No.5070 "Sir Daniel Gooch" makes a fine sight at Stafford Road, Wolverhampton, where the broad gauge ran out for both the GWR and OWW.
                                                                                         (T.E.Williams, National Railway Museum)

Old Worse & Worse?

With its main route complete and traffic growing, the OWW seemed set for expansion and a measure of prosperity. However, it was decided early in 1855 to terminate the contract of C.C.Williams with effect from 1st February 1856, by reason of 'excessive locomotive expenses'. David Joy, having been appointed by Williams, left at the same time.

Was the nickname "Old Worse & Worse" justified, was it even in use during the line's independent existence? Certainly there were derailments, mishaps and sloppy working practices. Such adventures were regularly mentioned in Joy's diary and there may well have been others that were not. Yet, apart from the appalling accident at Round Oak, which happened two years after Joy's departure, the early years also saw the gradual emergence of a railway that was beginning to take itself seriously. At a time when some directors were still fantasising about a London extension, professional railwaymen were determined to run the real railway to the best of their ability. Joy led the workforce by example. Having made a supreme effort to obtain four locomotives so that the line could open on time, he soon ordered others. By the end of 1852 the OWW had a growing stud of engines, two basic types for all needs. They look primitive to our eyes, but in the 1850s they were the latest proven technology and Joy was determined that they should earn their keep. He did not just write amusing accounts about misadventures on the line, his diary also contains informative statistics. His efforts to promote efficient fuel consumption have already been mentioned, but he also compiled a table of passenger train speeds, selecting from "Bradshaw" the times for the fastest trains on roughly fifty mile sections of other main lines. On home ground, between Handborough and Worcester, the fastest train in 1854 needed 1 hour 25 minutes for the journey, with four station stops. This could stand comfortably alongside the London & Brighton (1hr.20min. non-stop), LNWR (1hr.20min. Euston-Wolverton, non-stop), Great Western (1hr.5min. Paddington-Didcot, broad gauge, non-stop) and LSWR (1hr.20min. Waterloo-Basingstoke, non-stop). Joy noted that *"our speeds bore a very good comparison with anything else"*. He went on to produce figures for the first six months of 1854, showing the average mileage for every loco in six railway companies. Acquiring and processing such information was only for the dedicated and determined professional - some would say for the 'anorak' - but the statistics prove the point. The OWW had 28 engines, which had run 308,206 miles, an average of 11,007 miles per engine. Only the Manchester Sheffield & Lincoln squeezed more work out of its engines, an average of 11,608 miles for each of its 117 machines. All other companies had inferior results - Caledonian engines averaged 9,761 miles, followed by the South-Eastern (8,203 miles), Edinburgh Dundee & Perth (7,048) and Edinburgh & Glasgow (6,914).

Relations with the Great Western were undeniably poor, but they never broke down entirely. The two companies shared the main line and station at Wolverhampton without apparent difficulty. The OWW's Euston service was symbolic of the power and prejudice of a few directors, notably Parson, yet even these trains generally had good connections with Paddington at Oxford.

The best evidence of the efficiency of the OWW at this time comes from the valuation of rolling stock when Williams' contract was to be terminated. This was a lengthy process, begun in March 1855, and the figures were arrived at by a team of arbitrators, although W.E.MacConnell of the LNWR, supposedly acting for the OWW, may not have been entirely impartial. It seems he wanted to prove the point that there were 'excessive locomotive expenses', but he ended up proving the opposite. He ordered, for example, that an old 'Jenny', No.31, should have its firebox drilled because he thought it had worn thin - the drill proved otherwise. The valuation table, published from Joy's diary in the "Railway Magazine" in 1908, itemises all the rolling stock, valuing it at £183,205, which was £22,909 more than the £160,296 originally paid for it, as represented by Williams's invoices. This could only be the result of the care and maintenance it received in day to day running, even though the facilities at Worcester were barely complete by 1855. No wonder Joy wrote "Hurrah" at the foot of the table. He left Worcester and returned to the Railway Foundry at Leeds where, before turning to railways again, he busied himself with designs for marine engines and an early traction engine. He also patented a design for a hydraulic organ blower, examples of which powered the intruments in Leeds Town Hall and the Crystal Palace.

Joy was succeeded by Frederick Hayward, but was it as simple as that? It is not always easy to obtain an accurate picture of events that happened so long ago, often described by people who may not have been impartial. Hayward, for instance, is referred to as Mr.Haward in OWW minutes, which discussed his duties as resident assistant to John Gooch, Locomotive Superintendent, in November 1853, so where does that leave Joy? In January 1855, Joy was said to be in charge of the northern section of the line, Hayward of the southern (perhaps both were deputies to the seemingly low-profile Gooch?) and in June he applied for the post of Locomotive Superintendent (had Gooch retired?), only to be turned down. Although the facts are clouded, some things remain more clear. Extracts from Joy's diary were published verbatim in the "Railway Magazine", not noted for its bias, during 1907-08. Although it is obvious that his diary was 'written up' some while after events occurred, it was compiled from jottings in his note-book, in which he recorded events as soon as they happened. Intriguingly, he did not actually write, in April 1852 that he had been appointed Locomotive Superintendent, but that everything was *"arranged straight off"*. In any event, it is clear that his duties took him over the whole line and placed him in charge of the motive power, making him locomotive superintendent in fact even if not, maybe, in title. His own account comes through to me as essentially honest, giving an interesting and, I believe, reasonably accurate picture of the early OWW.

Hayward did become Locomotive Superintendent and ordered further locomotives from the Railway Foundry. The OWW continued to expand, as the stud of engines grew and plans for branch lines took shape. But technology remained primitive and the will to use it properly was often weak. There was as yet no proper means of locking signals and points together, thus preventing them from working against each other. A moment's carelessness by any signalman had the potential for disaster. Joy had recalled one occasion, in the winter of 1854-55, when a coal train was approaching Droitwich from Kidderminster with a clear road when, without warning, the signal reverted to danger. Joe Ludham was in charge of the train, one of a select band of young men who drove their engines hard and fast at every opportunity and who were collectively named 'Hell Fire Dick' by Joy. Ludham saw a mail train approaching from Stoke Works and, as there was no time for an emergency stop before the junction, accelerated furiously and attracted the attention of the driver of the mail. That man braked in the only way then possible, by using the reversing lever, and Ludham sped through the junction ahead of him.

An early photograph of a E.B.Wilson outside frame 0-6-0, bearing the initials of the West Midland Railway. The number is not apparent, but this was one of four engines (OWW Nos.27-30) delivered in 1854, one of which, No.29, was not scrapped until 1907.

(National Railway Museum)

OWW 0-6-0 No.33, delivered from Leeds 1855, scrapped 1885, seen here as GWR No.279.

(National Railway Museum)

The line was equipped with the telegraph, a useful aid to safe working that was not properly exploited. Train crews rarely knew the whereabouts of any permanent way gangs, so encounters could be dangerously unexpected. One evening in 1853, with Joy on the leading footplate of a double-headed 22-carriage special to Oxford, he admitted that, *"they had sent no notice down the line of our coming. It was a lovely summer evening. Suddenly slipping under a bridge the other side of Evesham at about 35 miles per hour, we saw the road lifted 8 inches both sides, a longish sleeper under it; there was but time to whistle the men away, and go on to await the result. We went up, then down, like a horse over a gate, and then turned as we stood on the tender to see if all else were also as lucky"*, which they were, the whole train following, stirred but intact.

Round Oak

With such working practices in common use during and after Joy's time, there was, somewhere, an accident waiting to happen. The disaster of Monday 23rd August 1858 caused a greater loss of life than any previous railway accident in Britain. An excursion train returning from Worcester to Wolverhampton split at Round Oak station. The rear 17 carriages, with about 450 people on board, ran back down the 1:75 incline and smashed into a following train. Fourteen passengers were killed and about fifty were seriously injured, with a further 170 applying for compensation because of injury to themselves or damage to their clothing.

The Accident Report, a copy of which was consulted by the author at the National Railway Museum, was compiled by Captain H.W.Tyler (Royal Engineers), and published on 16th October 1858. It describes the ways in which casual attitudes and working practices contributed to the disaster.

The train was advertised as an excursion for teachers and children of schools along the route, with a bargain return fare of one shilling (5p) for adults and 6d (2^1/$_2$ p) for children. This was an offer many non-teachers and non-children felt unable to refuse, so that by the day of travel 1,506 tickets had been issued, more than half (767) to adults. At Princes End, for example, 266 adults and 60 children were booked.

The train left Wolverhampton at 9.21am. A second locomotive was attached and 8 carriages added at Brettell Lane and five more carriages were added at Hagley. (The opening date of Hagley station is uncertain but it seems to have been functioning on this day.) The train was now of monstrous proportions, double-headed, with 37 carriages and a guard's van at each end. During the course of the journey couplings between various carriages near the rear of the train gave way - at Brettell Lane, Hagley and Droitwich - and on each occasion one of the guards, Frederick Cook, made running repairs.

It seems curious that while the train was on falling gradients couplings should fracture near the rear, away from the greater pulling force exerted by the locomotive. There was, however, irregular behaviour by Cook, who allowed some passengers into his van, the last vehicle in the train, smoking and drinking with them. On his own admission, he even allowed one of them to operate the brake! It was not, in such circumstances, worked responsibly or in co-ordination with the train's other brakes and such use would have put undue strain on the couplings. Four people were acting as brakesmen on the descent from Round Oak to Stourbridge. The guards in the front and rear were aided by two men, neither of them guards, in vans elsewhere in the train. There was Harris, an assistant from the superintendent of the line's office, who was in charge of the train south of Dudley, and

a bank engine foreman. Side chains complimented the couplings and four of these failed too. At Worcester, Harris reported a coupling fracture, just one. The rolling stock inspector confirmed four broken side chains, which were repaired, and three broken screw couplings, which were not, because he thought that the work would be too difficult in the confined space of the sidings. He considered the goods coupling links stronger than the screw couplings and that *"in the way in which they were fastened the train might travel safely back to Wolverhampton"*

For the return trip, mainly against the grade, one train became two. The first, with 28 carriages, was double-headed north of Stourbridge. The second had 14 carriages and both trains had a guard's van at each end, Frederick Cook in the rear van of the first train. As it was standing in Round Oak station a coupling gave way and the rear 17 carriages began to roll backwards. A platelayer on the other platform saw this, alerted the train crews (only the fireman of the second loco had noticed anything, a slight jerk), grabbed a lamp and chased in vain after the carriages. The booking clerk telegraphed Brettell Lane, Stourbridge and Kidderminster in a frantic attempt to alert them to the runaway but *"he was unable to gain attention from the clerks at those stations"*. The carriages ran back towards Moor Lane bridge, where they were seen by the driver of the second train, which was toiling up the 1:75 at about 10 miles per hour. By the time of the impact, south of the bridge, he had brought his train almost to a stand, making this a case of an unstoppable force meeting an immovable object, as the last three carriages shattered against the front of the locomotive. Because of the extent of the damage it was later calculated that the runaway must have been travelling at almost 18mph. Larger pieces of the smashed carriages were used as stretchers, smaller pieces were made into bonfires so that rescuers could see what they were doing, a nearby pub became a mortuary and - according to some press reports - the police were soon having to intervene to stop some local people from robbing the dead and unconscious. All the fatalities and most of the seriously injured were in the first train, although the shock of the impact rippled so violently through the second that the rear guard was knocked from one end of his van to the other.

Frederick Cook stated in evidence that once his train had split he had tried to apply the brake, yelling at the passengers to save themselves by jumping out, only abandoning his van just before impact. Given his earlier behaviour, Captain Tyler was not inclined to believe this. Cook said that before the impact the brake was working perfectly. Tyler organised a series of tests, on the same stretch of line, with an 'experimental train' of identical length, weighted as though it were full of passengers. It was allowed to run freely a number of times but each time the brake was applied, at various locations, it stopped well short of the accident site. Tyler also examined the wreckage of Cook's van, discovering that the nut which had been working on the brake screw had not been 'screwed down' to the bottom of the thread, which was still moist with oil. Therefore, the brake could not have been on when the crash occurred. When confronted with this, Cook lost what little credibility he had by saying that he released the brake at the moment before impact but, as Tyler wrote, *"It would be impossible to assign any reasonable motive for such a proceeding; and I can only suppose that he gave this piece of evidence in order to account for the condition in which the break screw remained"*. Tyler believed it probable that Cook had stepped from his van at Round Oak, without securing the brake, and the train had split after the buffers rebounded when it stopped. Unable to get back on board, he had followed the runaway on foot, perhaps managing to clamber onto the side of one of the carriages. Soon after the collision he was seen giving what assistance he could.

Round Oak station, looking north through the footbridge and Dudley Road, pannier tank on the 1:75 incline with a stopping train to Stourbridge, about 1960. *(John Dew; Ned Williams collection)*

2-6-2 tank No.4179 coasts down the gradient into Round Oak with the 3.57pm Wolverhampton-Stourbridge train, 16th June 1962.
(G.E.S.Parker, Kidderminster Railway Museum)

No fault was found with the couplings that would have caused them to fail in normal use, which they clearly did not receive on this occasion. Cook was criticised for his conduct on the train and the OWW was reprimanded for being apparently unaware of his character and that they were *"appointing a careless man, as he proves clearly to have been, to such important duties"*. He had served eight years as a goods guard, working the occasional summer excursion, while the guard in the front van normally worked as a porter. These men should not have been employed in this way, two brake vans for 28 carriages were insufficient, *"and such a proportion of controlling influence as that which could be exercised by two guards, with their own peculiar duties to attend to, is equally inadequate for keeping 1,000 pleasure-seeking excursionists in order"*.

Arrangements for the use of the telegraph proved totally useless in this emergency. The log book at Round Oak, in which all train movements should have been recorded, had not been used for three weeks because it was full and a new one was going to be ordered at the end of the month!

Between the accident and publication of the report, the OWW decided to install an early form of continuous vacuum braking system, Sander's Automatic, on all its passenger trains, whereby both sections of the train would stop automatically if it became divided. Captain Tyler commented favourably on this decision and concluded his report by criticising other companies *"that are in the daily habit of running passenger trains without any break vans at all behind them"*. Round Oak was a disaster, but it seems that some companies enjoyed greater luck than the OWW.

Expansion and Absorption

Less than a year after the OWW main line was authorised, an Act was passed on 27th July 1846 allowing construction of a branch from Honeybourne to Stratford-upon-Avon. Other branches followed, as will be seen in the next chapter, but the greatest leap forward came in 1860. On 14th June that year the OWW absorbed the Newport Abergavenny & Hereford (NA&H) and the Worcester & Hereford to form the West Midland Railway. Leap it really was, in the sense that there was a gap between the OWW and NA&H, as the Worcester & Hereford line was still incomplete.

The NA&H was a small and vulnerable system only 52 miles long. It was being bullied by a dispute with the LNWR, which would not allow its traffic to the north over the direct route through Shrewsbury. The NA&H was not cowed and cancelled its agreement with Euston. Very brave, but it still needed another outlet for its freight, chiefly South Wales coal. The directors appealed to the OWW, across the gap, for help. The result was co-operation and real benefits for all three companies - funds were injected into the Worcester & Hereford so that it could be completed (in 1861) and the NA&H could then re-route some traffic. In the amalgamation of 1860, as the OWW had 16 of the 23 directors (NA&H 5, W&H 2) and as the company headquarters remained at Worcester, the West Midland was an enlarged OWW in all but name.

The West Midland was absorbed by the GWR just three years later, on 1st August 1863. Conditions had become increasingly favourable for this logical move over the previous decade. The Great Western had taken over the Shrewsbury & Birmingham and the Shrewsbury & Chester railways in 1854. Both had been built to the standard gauge, but the sky did not fall in. A Northern Division was created at Wolverhampton and in 1859 two standard gauge locomotives were built at Stafford Road, the first of many hundreds. With an increased mileage of standard gauge track of its own the Great Western attitude to the OWW was bound to change. Hostilities diminished to the extent that by February

1858 the GWR agreed that the OWW could abandon its broad gauge rails. The necessary Act, cancelling out the relevant clauses of the 1845 Act, was passed in February 1859. The OWW was required to pay £2,000 per annum to the GWR for nine years and - no doubt causing wry smiles in both camps - much of the payment was in kind, in the form of surplus broad gauge rails!

John Parson's attitude remained unaltered but, as OWW directors retired or died, others with a more pragmatic approach replaced them. Now living in the past, even as the West Midland was formed, he revived a scheme for a London extension, pompously titled the "London, Buckinghamshire & West Midland Junction Railway". His force of personality and dictatorial manner, and the lingering attraction of a line to London, ensured that a Bill was submitted to Parliament in 1861. However, the directors finally woke up to the futility of the scheme and, without Parson's knowledge, approached the Great Western with a view to amalgamation. Terms were agreed on 4th May and the Bill was withdrawn. Amalgamation was not immediate, but planned for 1863, a diplomatic breathing space designed to assure the Midland Railway that there was no hostile intent - the Midland had running rights between Worcester and Hereford for access to its lines in South Wales. It was anxious to keep those rights, which it did.

The amalgamation, authorised by an Act of 13th July 1863, was effective from 1st August. With it the Great Western filled in the gap on its map between the Bristol and Birmingham main lines. It gained 339 route miles, 131 locomotives, 305 passenger carriages and 4,220 freight vehicles. The "Great Western Railway Magazine", in its regular column "The Month of the Rail", anticipated absorption of the West Midland (and certain minor lines in South Wales) by calculating the percentage distribution of future income to four decimal places - *"The receipts of the united concern, after deducting working expenses, interest on loans, and all other charges, will be divided between the several proprietaries, in the following proportions:- From 1st August 1863 to 31st January 1866 inclusive - Great Western 73.6725 : West Midland 15.6275 : South Wales 10.7000"*. All this long before the advent of pocket calculators, a nightmare for some unfortunate underpaid ledger clerks.

The West Midland Chairman, William Fenton, became deputy chairman of the GWR and six other WM directors, even including John Parson, joined the board. True to character, that sad individual was suspected of continued involvement in dubious financial activities. The scandal over a land deal in which he was implicated compelled him to resign in March 1864 after which, mercifully, his name ceased to feature in the history of the line.

A saddle tank calls at Moreton-in-Marsh with a train for Oxford, about 1895. The Shipston branch curves off to the right, behind the gents' urinal, with its decorated metal panels.   *(Author's collection, courtesy of CLPG)*

The original OWW engine shed at Kidderminster in a dilapidated condition, just before demolition in 1932. Both tracks in the foreground led to a turntable. The station signal box (left) was opened in 1882 and lasted until 1973. The 30-lever frame, by McKenzie & Holland of Worcester, is now in use at Arley box.   *(courtesy of Kidderminster Library)*

The 'Hare,' a locomotive borrowed from the Shrewsbury and Hereford Railway by the Oxford, Worcester and Wolverhampton Railway in January, 1853. Built by Bury in 1848. Cylinders, 16"×20"; Driving wheels, 6' 6" diameter; Heating surface, 1,217 sq. ft.

An illustration from the "Railway Magazine", 1907, showing early borrowed motive power on the OWW. *(author's collection)*

Worcester Shrub Hill before the overall roof was removed in 1938, with a long local train for the Hereford line, hauled by a 4-4-0 "Bulldog", signalled to depart from the bay platform. *(Author's collection)*

Worcester Shrub Hill, with "Saint" Class No.2973 "Robins Bolitho" on a stopping train. People share the platform with milk churns and a leaf spring on a barrow. The overall roof is receiving some attention. 1st August 1927. *(Kidderminster Railway Museum)*

6810 "Blakemere Grange", with an up express at Shrub Hill, is partially hidden by a 2-6-0 freight of the 4300 Class, No.5323, 6th July 1953. *(John Mudge)*

3440 "City of Truro", with congested footplate, leaves Worcester Shrub Hill for Kidderminster and the Severn Valley Railway, 9th September 1991. Great Western enthusiasts claim that "City of Truro" was the first loco to be reliably timed at over 100mph, in 1904, although on that occasion it would not have been hauling Mark I stock in Network South East livery! *(David Gomersall)*

A view of Worcester taken during World War II. The OWW sheds and the coaling stage lie between the OWW line (left) and the line to Foregate Street. To the left is Worcester works. *(Selwyn Pearce-Higgins, Jim Clemens collection)*

Inter-company co-operation at wartime Worcester. The LNER loco No.2051 is a Class J 25 0-6-0 freight, an 1898 design for the North Eastern Railway by T.W.Worsdell. *(Jim Peden collection)*

Worcester shed area, seen from Railway Walk during the ASLEF strike, 13th June 1955. An ex-Great Western diesel railcar, plus trailer, has left Shrub Hill bound for Malvern, worked by NUR staff perhaps? *(John Mudge)*

A general view of Worcester shed, 27th August 1961. Part of the works, the blacksmiths and fitting shops, are visible to the left, with the main line running between them and the OWW passenger shed (left centre). The larger OWW goods engine shed lies to the right, with Heenan & Froude, formerly the railway signalling works of McKenzie & Holland, to the rear. Locos in the picture include ex Great Western Nos.2867, 8107, 6335 and 6993. *(Michael Mensing)*

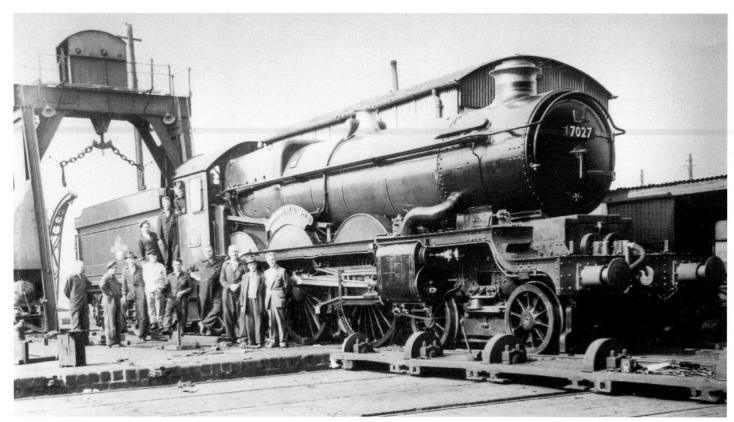

7027 "Hartlebury Castle" at Worcester works, standing between the hoist and traverser, about 1960. The locomotive is no more, but one nameplate is displayed in the entrance hall of the Worcestershire County Museum, which shares Hartlebury Castle with the official home of the Bishop of Worcester. *(Stephen Widdowson collection)*

5917 "Westminster Hall" and 0-4-2T No.5816 - under the hoist and with coupling rods removed - receive attention at Worcester works, 1956. *(Roger Carpenter collection)*

THE OWW IN COLOUR : PART ONE

47 706, still in Scot Rail livery, stands at Oxford's new station with a service for Paddington, 20th July 1991. *(Stephen Widdowson)*

47 040 arrives at Charlbury with a Paddington-Worcester Shrub Hill train, 16th February 1980. The length of the platform, or lack of it, is obvious.
(Steve Burdett)

A 'heritage' dmu passes Shipton Mill with the 06.04 Reading-Worcester Shrub Hill one clear spring morning, 24th April 1987.
(Stephen Widdowson)

An HST set approaches Moreton-in-Marsh with the 15.35 Paddington-Worcester, 25th July 1993. The train is nearing the end of the last remaining section of double track on the Cotswold Line, eleven miles between Ascott-under-Wychwood and Moreton. *(Andrew Bell)*

A 2-4-0 'Metro' tank has just brought a busy train of clerestory carriages into Witney, 1890s. The uniform smartness of the people, not an obviously third-class passenger in sight, suggests that this was some sort of special. The ladies' hats had not yet flowered into full Edwardian extravagance. The signal box, which appears to be of a standard GWR length (18 feet), was opened in 1892 and extended by about 7½ feet in 1898.   *(Author's collection)*

A member of the 7400 Class of pannier tanks (introduced 1936), No.7411, waits at Fairford with the 09.08 to Oxford, 6th August 1950. There is a wealth of interest here including (right to left) the ancient signal post, the pagoda shelter on the platform, the distinctive squat signalbox, the goods shed and the engine shed in the left distance - the nearest this branch ever got to its intended destination of Cheltenham.   *(John Edgington)*

been simpler just to bore the tunnel, but the spoil above was needed for the embankment nearer Stourport. The cutting can still be seen from the bridge on Wilden Top Road, sixty feet deep, damp and filled with mature trees. Victoria Bridge at Arley is an impressive piece of engineering, seen at its best from the footpath beneath, spanning the Severn in an elegant 200 foot leap. Its 500 tons look almost weightless, although each of the 36 cast iron segments that make up the arch weighs 7 tons. All were cast at the Coalbrookdale Iron Company, brought downriver, erected, bolted together and bound with wrought iron bracing.

Even before the line opened it had become obvious that the junction at Hartlebury would be inadequate, because it only faced Worcester. This was rectified with the opening of the Kidderminster-Bewdley loop on 1st June 1878. Bewdley, which had been a junction since the opening of the Tenbury branch in 1864, now had three platforms. The through tracks, between the north and south signal boxes, qualified as more than just a passing loop, making this the only double track on the SVR.

The line was seen as having considerable potential for freight. At the time its Act was passed in 1853, the china works at Coalport employed 700 people, Coalbrookdale Ironworks employed 4,000, with a further thousand working in Stourport's carpet factories. All these industries, and other later ones, benefited from the arrival of the railway. Alveley Colliery was rail served for the whole of its brief life (1939-1969). There was also an unadvertised halt for the miners. The sugar beet factory at Foley Park (1925-2002) continued to use rail until 1982. 75% of the beet arrived by rail in 1925 dropping to 56% by 1930.

But it is for leisure that this, the longest OWW branch, is chiefly known. By 1890 Bewdley and Stourport were gearing themselves up as tourist towns, with tea shops, boarding houses and river trips, all depending on the railway to bring in the necessary visitors. During the early twentieth century some Black Country people, often fishermen, built inexpensive cottages of wood, some little bigger than large sheds, on the banks of the Severn. They and their families escaped here whenever they could, by train. The biggest concentration of these buildings, still very much used and cared for, is at Northwood, where the GWR opened a halt in June 1935. For just one season, 1938, another sort of 'cottage' - a six-berth camping coach - was stabled at Arley, available to rent, for those arriving by train, at £3 per week.

Leisure also helped kill off the old SVR as, during the 1950s, the growing number of motorists had no reason to use the line, which could no longer be sustained by the local population alone. Closure came with the running of the last 'fisherman's special', a regular through train to Birmingham, on Sunday 8th September 1963. (A sparse passenger service continued to run on the Bewdley-Kidderminster-Hartlebury triangle until 3rd January 1970.)

But leisure revived the line too, as a core group of just eleven people met, at the suggestion of Keith Beddoes, at a private home in Kidderminster on 25th June 1965. They had the foresight to see the railway as a potential tourist attraction and, at their instigation, a public meeting took place in Kidderminster on 6th July, attended by about fifty people, at which it was decided to form the Severn Valley Railway Society. It was agreed to raise money and approach BR with a cash offer. The demolition train was travelling south and emerged from Bridgnorth tunnel on 24th July. Track removal in the station area began next day but frantic efforts by the volunteers, including a desperate telegram to BR Headquarters, and the positive response by BR to a group of amateurs who had yet to prove themselves, halted the demolition - permanently.

The SVR was incorporated on 24th May 1967. The number of volunteers grew steadily and now stands at over one thousand, of both sexes and all ages, including a growing number born well after the 1968 end of main line steam. Public services began between Bridgnorth and Hampton Loade on 23rd May 1970, and were then extended south, reaching Bewdley in May 1974 and Kidderminster Town on 30th July 1984. The new terminus is on the site of Kidderminster goods yard and the buildings, which opened in September 1985, are to an 1890 design for the station at Ross-on-Wye. The company had to provide bridges over the by-passes at Bridgnorth (1983) and Bewdley (1986). An engine shed and workshop are located at Bridgnorth and a 1/3 mile long four-road carriage shed was opened at Kidderminster in 2000. It cost £2.25 million, 75% met from the Heritage Lottery Fund, the remainder by SVR shareholders.

The Severn Valley today is more than just a railway, in fact it is no longer even a railway in its original sense, as nobody depends on it to get about. The wide programme of events - Santa specials, 1940s weekends, steam and diesel galas, Thomas the Tank Engine, etc. etc. - mark it as an important tourist attraction. The immaculate stations, authentic restoration of the signalling etc., and the wide variety of resident and visiting locomotives mean that the line is helping preserve our railway history in a living and lively way. John Fowler could not have imagined the traffic his Victoria Bridge carries in the twenty-first century, but he would certainly approve.

Table 155 **OXFORD, WITNEY and FAIRFORD**

Miles	Week Days only — HOUR →		pm 12 (2)	4	6	9 E	10 E	pm 10 S
—	**Oxford**	dep	15	18	18	50	.	10
3¾	Yarnton		23	26	26	58	.	18
5	Cassington Halt		27	30	30	**3**	.	23
7¼	Eynsham		33	37	36	9	.	29
9¼	South Leigh		39	43	42	15	.	35
12	**Witney**	arr	44	48	48	20	.	40
		dep	49	54	56	.	26	46
15¾	Brize Norton & Bampton		**2**	**3**	**5**	.	35	55
17	Carterton		6	8	10	.	39	59
17¾	Alvescot		10	12	14	.	43	**3**
20¼	Kelmscott & Langford		16	19	21	.	49	9
22¼	Lechlade		22	26	28	.	55	15
25½	**Fairford**	arr	29	33	35	.	**2**	22

Miles	Week Days only — HOUR →		am 6	8 (2)	12	1 (2)	2 (2)	pm 6
—	**Fairford**	dep	47	.	10	55	.	10
3¼	Lechlade		55	.	18	**3**	.	19
5¼	Kelmscott & Langford		**0**	.	23	8	.	24
7¾	Alvescot		6	.	29	14	.	30
8½	Carterton		10	23	33	18	.	35
9¾	Brize Norton & Bampton		15	28	38	23	.	39
13½	**Witney**	arr	22	35	45	30	.	47
		dep	28	43	**0**	.	40	**4**
16¼	South Leigh		33	48	5	.	45	9
18¼	Eynsham		38	54	10	.	50	14
20½	Cassington Halt		45	**1**	17	.	57	20
21¾	Yarnton		49	5	21	.	**1**	23
25½	**Oxford**	arr	56	13	28	.	8	30

E Except Saturdays, **S** Saturdays only **(2)** Second class only

OTHER TRAINS between Oxford and Yarnton, see Table 163

From 'Bradshaw's Railway Guide' for December 1958-March 1959. *(courtesy of Gordon Park)*

A Midland & South-West Junction Rly 2-4-0 poses for the camera with a blanket train at Witney goods shed. The 'MSWJ' cypher is visible and the company was absorbed by the GWR in the 1923 Grouping, around the time of this photograph.

(Oxfordshire County Council Photographic Archive)

End of the line at Fairford, with 5413 (left) and 7411 on shed, 31st July 1954. 7411 will collect the stock to form the next train to Oxford.

(C.H.A.Townley, Jim Peden collection)

0-6-2T No.6696 enters Kidderminster yard with a train of sugar beet, 30th October 1960. The refinery was situated at Foley Park and opened in 1925. It was rail served until 22nd January 1982 and closed completely on 25th January 2002. The yard is now partly occupied by the Severn Valley Railway's turntable (1994) and carriage shed (2000). *(Brian Moone, Kidderminster Railway Museum)*

Bewdley station, looking towards Bridgnorth, about 1890, with what is probably a Wolverhampton built 517 Class 0-4-2 tank engine at the head of a soutbound train, with tops of the lamp wells visible on the carriage roofs. Even the dog is interested in the camera.

(Museum Service, Wyre Forest District Council)

0-6-0 tank No.9656 calls at Northwood Halt with a southbound train from Bridgnorth, 6th February 1960.

(G.E.S.Parker, Kidderminster Railway Museum)

Two golfers search for a missing ball, oblivious to the train. 4129 heads a northbound coal freight, one mile north of Bridgnorth, 30th August 1962.

(Michael Mensing)

The Stourbridge Extension

The Stourbridge Railway was responsible for this line and for an early attempt to build the branch to Stourbridge Town, for which a separate Act was passed in 1865. With no rolling stock of its own, it could only be nominally independent, like so many small companies. It was entirely reliant on the West Midland and later the GWR, in order to function at all, and it was absorbed by the GWR in 1871. The Stourbridge Extension is the most important branch off the OWW main line. It gives Stourbridge, Kidderminster and a string of lesser industrial towns - Lye, Cradley Heath, Old Hill, Rowley - direct links with the Birmingham lines of both the LNWR and GWR, with passenger services to both New Street and Snow Hill. The original Act of 1860, which also brought into being the West Midland Railway, only authorised construction between Stourbridge and Cradley Heath, but the Stourbridge Railway Extension Act of 1861 sanctioned the rest, to join the LNWR at Galton Junction. The short link beyond there, to the GWR at Handsworth Junction, was authorised in 1862.

The line opened to Cradley, with an intermediate station at Lye, on 1st April 1863. It was operated briefly by the West Midland Railway, for just four months before it was absorbed by the Great Western. There were eight trains in each direction, taking ten minutes for the 2¼ mile journey. The service was extended to Old Hill on New Year's Day 1866 and the whole route was open on 1st April 1867. At Lye - which used to be known as 'bucket capital of the world' - the goods yard was busy, for the next hundred years, with the dispatch of galvanised buckets, baths, dustbins, etc. The process of galvanising metal with a protective coating of zinc is generally thought to have been developed at Lye by George Hill, aged 18, in 1863.

The junction at Stourbridge was at the northern end of the station platforms on a tight curve. Like the OWW north of Stourbridge, the Extension has steep northbound gradients, stiffening to 1:51 for 1½ miles at Old Hill. As the number and length of freight trains grew, on the main line and on the Extension, there was an increasing amount of work for banking engines. The GWR opened Stourbridge's first shed in 1870, west of the main line and north of the junction. In 1901, 36 of its 42 locos were tank engines, all muscle and brawn for banking and short haul freight. The shed was replaced in 1926 by what proved to be the last GWR roundhouse, but continued in use for steam rail motors and diesel railcars.

Stourbridge Town

The Act for construction of this Great Western branch was passed on 30th June 1874 and the line opened to passengers on 1st May 1879. The 'County Express' reported (4th May) *"This branch has been the subject of perpetual agitation for some years past, owing to the inconvenience caused by the fact that the existing station ... was placed for some undiscoverable reason a long way from the centre of the town ... A commodious goods station is in course of erection in Mill Meadow ... Hitherto goods brought to this point have been carried to the main line by means of an inclined railway, up which trucks are drawn by rope to a stationary engine situated between the Stambermill Viaduct and Brettell Lane. This incline will now be done away with as will also the present goods station at Stourbridge Junction when the arrangements for the goods traffic are completed."* The 'inclined railway' had a gradient of 1:14, up which a maximum of four loaded trucks were normally hauled.

The new line, with its own formidable gradient of 1:27

beyond the passenger station, opened for freight on 1st January 1880 and there were hopes that it would be extended to Wordsley, Sedgley and Kinver. Such aspirations were expressed at the banquet at the Talbot Hotel on the day the passenger service started. There were no ceremonies to mark the departure of the first train, at 7.42am, which left *"under the eyes of few spectators"*, although more people rode the branch during the day as the weather became brighter.

'Stourbridge' became Stourbridge Junction and the branch station became 'Stourbridge' instead. Although known as Stourbridge Town from the beginning, it was not labelled as such until fitted with British Railways totems about 1957. The branch was worked as double track between the junction and town, with a signal box at the Town station, until 1935, after which it was worked as two parallel single lines, each on the 'one engine in steam' principle and controlled from Stourbridge Junction Middle Signal Box. The branch, as built, met the main line just south of the Junction station which, with two short platforms, had become inadequate. The present Junction station opened, to the south, in October 1901. It had four through platforms and branch activities no longer conflicted with movements on the main line. The connection was realigned, so trains coming off the branch faced south, rather than north, as they entered the new station. A large scale OS Map, surveyed during 1901, shows the branch tracks leading to the old junction station; it also shows the new alignment with track partly laid.

During the First World War the branch was closed to passengers with effect from 29th March 1915. That night the Borough Council unanimously passed a resolution protesting about it. As with many other small stations, wartime closure was undertaken to release men for military service. According to the "County Express" although it was from 'patriotic motives' only about eight people would be released from railway work, one a boy, another a cripple. *"Councillor Hall said he could not see where the military advantage was. Certainly there were not more than two employees of military age. Here was a case where ladies might come in"*. The men of Stourbridge may have been patriotic, but what about their manners? The discussion described how, when the branch train sometimes ceased after 6pm, to be replaced by buses (for reasons not mentioned in the report), a bus would arrive at the junction and there would be a scramble for it, *"the men got there first and filled the 'bus and the women had to walk."* The branch reopened on 1st May 1919.

The ruling gradient down from the junction is 1:67, with a 20mph speed limit. Beyond the town station the goods branch steepened to 1:27 for a quarter mile, ending where a footbridge spanned the entrance to the goods yard. Despite the gradient, and because train movements were rigorously controlled, there were only two runaways of note on the goods branch, in 1905 and 1948. The yard closed in July 1965 and the formation was cut back, ending in a brick wall overlooking Foster Street, just beyond the Town station. This was breached by the 'Town Car', in 1977, which was left hanging precariously over the road. The branch was later cut back and a new station provided. Trains overshot the end of the line again in 1989 and 1990, due to brake failure on the ageing 'bubble car' units. Nowadays a more modern (1987) Class 153 single unit shuttles to and fro over 75 times daily along what is probably the shortest branch line in the world, shorter than ever since 1994, as it was cut back again when the bus station was modernised and a new railway station built adjacent to it, almost as an extra bus bay.

A pannier tank struggles up the awesome 1:27 gradient from Stourbridge goods yard towards the Town station with the maximum permitted load, for the ascent, of ten vehicles. *(John Dew; Ned Williams collection)*

5754 nears the top of the climb from Stourbridge goods yard. The line is bridging Birmingham Street, near what is now the town's ring road. Across the fields, to the right, is Stourbridge engine shed. The goods yard is to the left of the train - thirty feet below and reached by a 1:27 descent - with wagons, road vehicles, footbridge spanning the site and the gasometer beyond.

(John Dew; New Williams collection)

The scene at the end of the Stourbridge Town goods branch on Easter Monday, 24th April 1905. A 0-6-0 saddle tank was descending the 1:27 incline, bunker first, with 32 laden wagons when it began to run out of control. The fireman left the cab as he and two yard shunters attempted to slow progress by applying the brakes on individual wagons and putting sprags in front of the wheels but it was in vain. Still travelling at about 10mph, the loco demolished the stop block and punched a hole in the wall of the empty goods office. Wagons piled up behind the engine, the first two coming to rest with buffers pointing skywards. The photograph, produced as a commercial postcard, shows removal of the leading wagon by crane. The two men on the left were, apparently, brothers of Joe Bache, a member of the Aston Villa team which beat Newcastle United 2-0 in the 1905 cup final. *(courtesy of Stourbridge Library)*

Stourbridge Town, spring 1957, as a pannier tank approaches the perilous descent to the goods yard beyond, a quarter of a mile at 1:27. The connection from the passenger line is permanently blocked by a van. The double deck Midland Red buses were once a familiar sight all over the region and Stourbridge still had a cinema (left). *(John Edgington)*

[Chapter Three continues on page 73]

THE OWW IN COLOUR ... PART TWO

A Class 150 Sprinter, in Centro livery, heads north past Tunnel Junction Signal Box, Worcester, 3rd February 1994. *(Andrew Bell)*

A contrast in liveries at Worcester Shrub Hill. A Thames turbo approaches with a Hereford-Paddington train, a Central Trains Class 170 waits on the centre road while, in the distance, there is a rake of Mark I stock in 'blood and custard' livery. March 2000.

(David Pagett)

Seen from a public footpath crossing the line, a Swindon-built Class 120 Cross Country dmu leaves Worcester's Rainbow Hill Tunnel with a Great Malvern-Birmingham New Street service, 22nd August 1976. *(Steve Burdett)*

In the days when some cross country InterCity trains called at Worcester Shrub Hill (lengthening their schedules by about twenty minutes), 47 244 approaches Rainbow Hill Tunnel with the 09.15 Birmingham New Street-Taunton, Sunday 29th May 1978. The site of Blackpole Halt, an unadvertised halt for workers' trains, open 1917-20 and 1940-46, lay at the rear of the train. *(Steve Burdett)*

Chiltern Clubman 168 112 at Stourbridge Junction with the 06.02 to Marylebone, 23rd May 2001. *(John Boynton)*

25 273 at Amblecote with a coal train for the Pensnett branch, 29th March 1976. Stambermill Viaduct, Stourbridge and the Clent Hills form the backdrop. *(Steve Burdett)*

An ex-LMS Class 2 Ivatt 2-6-2 tank, No.41209, leaves Bridgnorth behind with the 7.27pm to Shrewsbury, 8th June 1963.

(Michael Mensing)

0-6-0 No.3205, of the 2251 Class (later removed to Minehead) hauls a rare non-public passenger train on the Severn Valley Railway, prior to the launch of public services in May 1970. This is the scene south of Eardington on Easter Monday, 15th April 1968.

(Michael Mensing)

Ex-LMS 2-8-0 freight loco No.48773 approaches Victoria Bridge with the 2.50pm Bridgnorth-Kidderminster Town, 8th October 2000. The hint of autumn colour and a faint smudge of rainbow help make this a most attractive composition. *(Andrew Bell)*

7819 "Hinton Manor" near the site of the closed station at Eardington with the 5pm Kidderminster-Bridgnorth, 8th April 1987. Outshopped in unlined green by the GWR when new in 1939, it was painted in BR lined black by the SVR in 1985. *(Andrew Bell)*

A southbound empty stock train joins the main line at Kingswinford Junction, 26th August 1961. The locomotive is 6319 (4300 Class), a 1911 freight design by Churchward.
(Michael Mensing)

A hive of activity at Brierley Hill steel terminal, Kingswinford Junction, 27th October 1978. 47 334 leaves the busy yard with a southbound train, while another train lurks at the exit from the Pensnett branch.
(Steve Burdett)

5700 Class 0-6-0 pannier tank No.9674 arrives at Princes End & Coseley with the 11.07am Stourbridge Junction–Wolverhampton (L.L.), Sunday 30th July 1961. Many people in the Black Country were (and are) pigeon fanciers. Some of them wait on the soutbound platform for the arrival of a pigeon special, which was formed by diesel parcels car W55993 and a bogie parcels van. *(Michael Mensing)*

47 479 passes Blower's Green on a southbound freight, complete with period cars, 10th November 1976. *(Michael Mensing)*

Pannier tank No.6434 leaving Darby End Halt with the 7pm from Old Hill to Dudley, 14th May 1964. *(Michael Mensing)*

A Western Region Gloucester-built Class 122 bubble car meanders along the Bumble Hole line, south of Baptist End Halt, with the 5.25pm Dudley-Old Hill, 14th May 1964. *(Michael Mensing)*

The Kingswinford Branch

On 14th November 1858 the OWW opened a short goods branch from a new junction at Kingswinford, north of Brettell Lane, to connect with the busy canal basin at Bromley, less than a mile away. It was later extended northwards to connect with the Earl of Dudley's Railway, at Pensnett. During the nineteenth century the GWR drew up plans for a direct line between Wolverhampton and Bridgnorth, which are only 14 miles apart. No fewer than nine Bills were prepared between 1860 and 1904. Finally, an Act was passed in the 1905 session, authorising extension of the Kingswinford branch north, to a junction at Oxley, on the Wolverhampton-Shrewsbury line. Wolverhampton-Bridgnorth trains would use this route as far as Wombourn (the GWR dropped the 'e'), branching off on a new line which would join the Severn Valley just south of Bridgnorth station. Construction was slow and, so far as the Bridgnorth branch was concerned, it never began. Delayed by the First World War, the rest of the line did not open until 11th May 1925. A sparse service of steam rail motors flittered briefly through the delightful but thinly populated landscape. There were nine halts between Kingswinford and Oxley junctions and all trains ran between Wolverhampton and Stourbridge Junction, but only until 31st October 1932, when the service ceased. The Wombourn line continued as a freight and diversionary route until closure as a through line on 27th February 1965. The southern section was in use until about 1990, with a rail distribution depot at Pensnett, just north of the A4101. Kinswinford Junction itself remains the site of a steel terminal.

Netherton-Old Hill

In July 1862 the West Midland Railway secured an Act for this branch, which linked the OWW main line with the Stourbridge Extension, but it was not opened until 1st March 1878. The OWW station at Netherton was closed and replaced by a new one, 1/4 mile north, at the junction. It was known as 'Dudley (South Side) & Netherton' but the name was changed to a more easily digestible 'Blower's Green' in 1921. There was one intermediate station, at Windmill End. Throughout the line's existence all passenger trains ran to and from Dudley. There were also a few through workings to Birmingham Snow Hill via Old Hill. The train service was revolutionised in September 1905 with the introduction of steam railmotors, which ran at roughly hourly intervals, and the opening of basic wooden halts at Baptist End, Darby End and Old Hill (High Street). Despite the rural sounding names, this double track 3 mile branch, with north facing junctions at both ends and a ruling gradient of 1:53, passed through a heavily industrialised area. The line was known as the 'Bumble Hole'. By the 1950s the halts were literally disintegrating. Old Hill (High Street) was given new concrete platforms and shelters in 1956 after which, in its wisdom, the Western Region confined the train service to the peak hours, in the summer of 1958. Passenger numbers declined and, in the absence of any positive thinking, the line was an obvious candidate for closure. The last trains ran on 13th June 1964, although freight survived until the end of 1967.

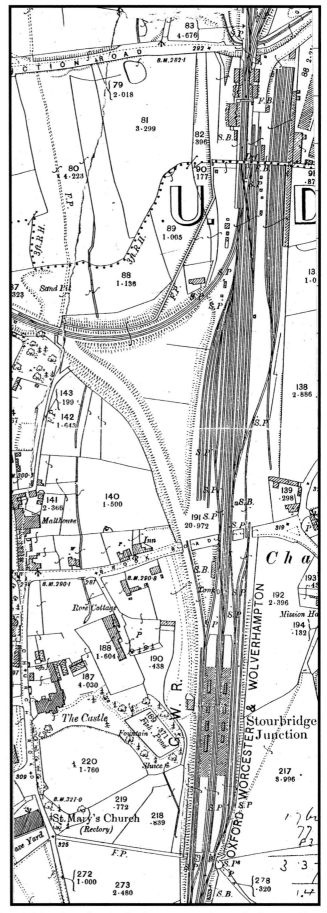

Large scale OS map surveyed in 1901, showing both stations at Stourbridge Junction (only the new one is marked as such) and the incomplete new connection with the Town branch.

(courtesy of Stourbridge Library)

The Stourbridge Extension Railway, a direct route to Birmingham, leaves the OWW at Stourbridge Junction. The junction itself was created by this line, the first section of which opened in 1863 between Stourbridge and Old Hill, with intermediate stations at Lye and Cradley. 5180 enters Lye with a stopping train from Birmingham Snow Hill, 1957. A large quantity of hollow-ware was received at the goods yard, seen here complete with travelling crane. To the left, off camera, was Orchard House (now used as offices), the home of George King Harrison, brick manufacturer. The coming of the railway saw the conversion of his secluded private drive into Station Road, with the station platforms laid virtually at his front door. *(John Edgington)*

Blower's Green on 12th June 1964 as 6434 propels its train round the curve onto the Bumble Hole line. The last Dudley-Old Hill trains ran on the following day.
(Peter Shoesmith; Ned Williams collection)

A forlorn line of pannier tanks at Stourbridge, just before closure of the shed, *(Brian Robbins)*

2-6-2 tank No.4161 arrives at Brettell Lane with the 4.55pm Wolverhampton Low Level-Stourbridge Junction, 11th June 1962. The footbridge gave direct access from the road to the small goods yard and shed. In the early twentieth century, when the electric tram service along Brettell lane was efficient and frequent, and the Stourbridge Town train was not, it was quicker and cheaper for people travelling between Wolverhampton and Stourbridge to use the tram between Brettell Lane station and the town centre. *(Michael Mensing)*

4179 arrives at Brierley Hill with the 6.20pm Worcester Shrub Hill-Wolverhampton Low Level, 26th August 1961. Brierley Hill Glassworks, the home of Royal Brierley Crystal, can be seen beyond the bridge carrying Moor Street. A siding is visible, where the raw materials for glassmaking - chiefly silver sand and potash - were received until the 1960s. The lead crystal was also dispatched by rail, in containers packed tightly with straw, which were locked and secured with lead seals. The GWR and the glassworks were rightly proud of the fact that breakages were virtually unknown.
(Michael Mensing)

A northbound grain train regaining the main line off the loop, north of Round Oak, 20 056 and 20 117 at the head, with 31 161 banking off camera. The line crosses the Pensnett Canal, Brierley Hill Ironworks forming a backdrop, 29th April 1986.
(Brian Robbins)

58 003 shunts a short container train at Dudley, c.1985.

(Brian Robbins; Ned Williams collection)

A 1965 photograph of the OWW line, between Dudley and Tipton, at the point where it passed over the Dudley No.1 Canal, with its entrance to the Tipton and Dudley canal tunnels. A British Railways scheme of 1964 to replace the railway bridge with an embankment, due to mining subsidence, met with stiff opposition from canal preservationists, as it would have meant filling in the waterway beneath the railway and blocking off the canal tunnels. The canal was saved and the site, one of the birthplaces of the Industrial Revolution, now forms part of the Black Country Living Museum. *(Richard Amott)*

7904 "Fountains Hall" arrives at the delapidated station of Princes End & Coseley with a return excursion from Malvern Wells to Wolverhampton, Whit Monday, 11th June 1962. *(Michael Mensing)*

5031 "Totnes Castle" approaches Priestfield station with the 2.35pm Worcester-Wolverhampton, 30th April 1960. The bridge carries Ward Street, which marked the boundary between Wolverhampton and Bilston, a Primitive Methodist chapel to the left, while Bilston Gas Works, rail-served from the OWW line, looms large in the middle distance. *(Michael Mensing)*

Feel the heat on a hot day in an exceptional summer. 4925 "Eynsham Hall" takes water at Wolverhampton Low Level, the one time northern limit of the OWW, 4th July 1959. The train is from Bournemouth to Birkenhead, although the ex-LNER Gresley corridor 1st - deep inside alien territory - is labelled 'Chester'. A carriage at the High Level station peeps above the parapet to the left.

(Michael Mensing)

Rusty and run down, end of steam, end of OWW line, as 6847 "Tidmarsh Grange" heads north past Cannock Road sidings, Wolverhampton, 24th July 1965.

(Brian Robbins)

CHAPTER FIVE : MODERN TIMES

[Diary : Change, Contraction and Closure : Progress and Revival]

Diary

1961

30th December : Closure proposal for Stourbridge-Wolverhampton announced in local press.

1962

31st May : D1000 "Western Enterprise" brand new and allocated to Stafford Road, hauls the 10.15 Wolverhampton-Worcester local train as a running in turn.

29th July : Last day of passenger services between Priestfield and Stourbridge Junction.

October : Ex-GWR diesel railcars withdrawn and replaced by new BR Class 122 'bubble cars'. Six railcars withdrawn from Worcester, with two briefly retained in reserve.

1963

23rd January : First main line diesel arrives at Worcester for crew training, D6518 (33 013).

9th May : A new diesel hydraulic Hymek loco, D7076, just three days out of the works, arrives at Worcester for crew training, plus two more Hymeks on loan from Old Oak Common and one from Cardiff Canton. Hymeks haul some Worcester-Paddington trains at the start of the summer time-table. One Hymek failure, on 12th August, meant that a Paddington-Worcester train was hauled by a 'Western' diesel, probably for the first time (D1068 "Western Reliance" on the 11.15 ex-Paddington and 15.10 return).

4th September : Last steam "Cathedrals Express" to Paddington, 7005 "Sir Edward Elgar".

9th September : Start of the winter time-table, which should have meant the total dieselisation of the Paddington-Worcester-Hereford service. Failures suffered by the Hymeks resulted in no fewer than 73 substitutions by steam during the first three weeks. Worcester's three remaining "Castles" were very active.

13th September : Four new English Electric type 3 diesels (Class 37) arrive at Worcester.

September : Wolverhampton Stafford Road shed closed.

1964

1st June : Honeybourne closed to goods traffic from this date.

13th June : Last day of passenger services on the 'Bumble Hole', Old Hill-Dudley.

8th August : Kidderminster shed closed. A number of drivers retired as a result *"and were presented with books on the history of ASLEF"* (Kidderminster Times, 14th August).

August : Three new Class 47 diesel locomotives arrive at Worcester for crew training.

4th September : Last steam local train at Worcester, from Snow Hill, hauled by a "County".

1st October : Worcester locomotive repair works closed.

3rd-4th October : Rail bridge installed over Worcester's new northern link road at Blackpole.

29th October : Worcester railway works closed.

1965

30th January : Funeral train of Sir Winston Churchill brought his body to Handborough.

3rd April : Last day of train services at Fernhill Heath and Cutnall Green Halt.

The start of the summer time-table in June brought to an end the Kidderminster portion of Worcester-Paddington trains, normally three carriages attached/detached at Shrub Hill.

December : Worcester shed closed to steam and converted to a stabling point only.

1966

1st January : Last day of train service for eight stations and halts on the Cotswold Line.

15th July : Rear coach of a Hereford-Paddington express derailed at Kingham, both lines blocked, fourteen casualties, none of whom sustained serious injuries.

During the summer of 1966 the last 'Jinty' tank engine to be built, No.47681, developed a hot box while passing through Worcester, en route to Newport for scrap. There was no point it repairing it so, after being stored briefly, it was cut up at Worcester.

1967

Fastest Worcester-Paddington train accelerated to 2 hours 5 mins for summer time-table.

16th July : Dudley Freightliner Terminal opened.

16th October : Sheet works at Worcester were gutted by fire.

1968

During the summer Kidderminster's station buildings were examined and found to have major structural defects. They were condemned and taken out of use. A temporary wooden booking office was erected on the station drive and construction of new station buildings, already planned, was brought forward. The Birmingham platform was shortened at the north end, the remainder raised to modern standard height. There was to be a new footbridge adjacent to the road bridge, but this was never built although included in the whole scheme, which was costed, according to a report in "Railway Magazine" at £60,000.

4th August : Worcester wagon works and its associated trackwork taken out of use.

1969

February : Worcester railway works demolished.

3rd May : Last day of services at Honeybourne.

13th July : Demolition began of the four OWW goods engine sheds at Worcester.

1974

6th May : Start of new time-table saw improvement to the service at Cotswold Line halts. A dmu served all stations Oxford-Moreton, leaving Oxford 08.52 and 13.02, leaving Moreton 10.12 and 14.02. The trains received little publicity and were withdrawn after a year.

1975

28th July : Train service at Pershore doubled, from one each way per day to two. Fourteen years later, in 1989, there was still a three-hour gap in trains in each direction in the middle of the day and the Town Council was reminding BR that, with a population of over 7,000, Pershore was the largest centre of population, apart from Evesham, along the Cotswold Line.

1978

11th March : Cotswold Line Promotion Group (CLPG) formed.

1981

22nd May : Honeybourne reopened. First train was 11.40 Shrub Hill-Paddington, hauled by 47 510 "Fair Rosamund" and greeted by a large number of flag waving schoolchildren and the brass band of Pershore High School. The station was decorated with bunting and the loco carried a headboard declaring "Honeybourne Station Is Back in Business".

1983

16th May : Improved passenger service Birmingham-Hereford, with benefits to Stourbridge-Worcester section of OWW.

A Birmingham Railway Carriage & Wagon built loco, D6533, based on the Southern Region, heads south through Fladbury with a train of Esso fitted tanks, presumably empties returning to Fawley, 18th May 1963. These 98 1550hp machines were built between 1959 and 1962, they were the first diesel electric locos to provide electric train heating exclusively, and later classified as Class 33. The double skinned cab roof is of moulded fibreglass and the two character headcode is normal for the Southern Region, where all these engines were based.   *(Michael Mensing)*

Echoes of times past as 5029 "Nunney Castle" enters Evesham, 27th June 1993. This was not the "Cathedrals Express" but a charter train returning to Didcot from Shrub Hill, although the headboard was genuine. Unfortunately, the lure of steam always brings out the worst in some people, like the idiot mother encouraging her child to trespass on the line.   *(Stephen Widdowson)*

1984

14th May : First HST on Cotswold Line, 10.25 Paddington-Great Malvern and 13.43 return.

1986

26th September : Dudley Freightliner Terminal closed.

1988

8th-10th October : Main line between Worcester and Norton Junction closed for the weekend to allow the installation of a new railway bridge over the Worcester southern link road (A4440), then under construction. Road contractors Monks had built the 800 tonne concrete bridge alongside the railway embankment. The whole structure rested on rails. The railway was closed at 13.00 on 8th, the track removed and JCB diggers brought in to remove the embankment. Removal was complete by 07.00 on Sunday, when huge jacks pushed the bridge into place, 50 metres in 5 hours. Line reopened at 11.00 on Monday 10th.

1989

OWW passenger engine shed at Worcester demolished during November-December.

1990

BR announced withdrawal of Pershore stop from 18.20 Paddington-Hereford from start of new time-table in May. Local people submitted a petition, with the support of the local council, MP and Bishop of Worcester. The reply by BR Chairman, Sir Robert Reid was less than tactful when he suggested that Pershore only needed four trains a day instead of the then-current twelve.

Colour light signals installed between Norton Junction and Shrub Hill in the winter of 1989/90.

New stabling point built at Worcester during the year.

3rd October : Ceremony at Oxford to mark completion of the rebuilding of the station. 47 547 named "University of Oxford", 47 587 named "Ruskin College Oxford". The station had been in use for six months but was officially opened by BR Chairman Sir Bob Reid (successor to Sir Robert Reid), his first official duty three days after taking up his appointment. The Oxford Mail headline, "Proud BR opens station but Lord Mayor nags", referred to criticisms made by Mayor Mrs.Queenie Hamilton on the lack of facilities for disabled passengers, such as lifts as an alternative to the footbridge. Lifts were eventually provided.

1993

21st February : First Class 165 two-car Turbo dmu arrived at Shrub Hill for crew training.

19th March : Last day Dudley-Stourbridge section of OWW used as a through freight route.

30th April : First Class 166 three-car Turbo dmu on the Cotswold Line, on a crew training run between Worcester and Oxford. The 166s entered service between Oxford and Hereford at the start of the new timetable on 17th May.

16th May : Last time-tabled loco hauled train over the Cotswold Line, the 15.37 (SuO) Paddington-Worcester. The loco was 47 821, carrying the "Cathedrals Express" headboard.

12th July : 12.48 Paddington-Worcester began calling at Pershore, plugging a four hour gap in the train service.

22nd August : Double Red on a Single Red route. 6024 "King Edward I" became probably the first 'King' to haul a train between Worcester and Oxford. The special had started at Wolverhampton at 08.30, worked to Oxford via Birmingham, then back to Shrub Hill before continuing to Didcot via Gloucester. The King's axle weight prevented use of the triangle for turning at Worcester, which would have included crossing the bridge over the Severn.

6th November : What was claimed to be the first electric bus service in the country was launched at Oxford station. The 'City Circuit' buses linked the station with the city centre and were plugged in to recharging points on the station forecourt.

1994

11th March : Closure notices published for Finstock and Combe halts, in accordance with terms of Section 56 (7) of the Transport Act of 1962. The stated reason for closure was that it would not be cost effective for the platforms to be improved to meet new safety standards but BR failed to notify the Health & Safety Executive of this. In May, due to these procedural errors the closure notice was declared null and void, so it would have to be published again. In the meantime, Section 56 (7) of the 1962 Act was repealed under terms of the 1993 Railways Act, effective from 1st April 1994. No new closure notice was issued and the halts remain open.

1996

26th July : New expanded steel terminal opened at Wolverhampton on the same approximate site as the OWW Walsall Street goods depot.

1999

27th June : The rebuilt "Flying Scotsman" locomotive, still in grey undercoat and on its first outing for three years, hauled a special on a round trip from Southall, travelling southbound from Birmingham Snow Hill via Stourbridge, Worcester and Oxford.

2000

Early in the year Railtrack double glazed the signal boxes on the Cotswold Line.

5th February : Meeting at County Hall, Worcester, to resurrect and progress the idea of a Worcester Parkway station. Those attending included county councillors, both local MPs, the Chief Executive of Virgin Rail, plus representatives of Railtrack, Central Trains and Wales & West. Great Western and Thames Trains did not send representatives.

18th May : First appearance of Class 170 dmu at Worcester, when 170 630, with special guests on board, ran from Shrub Hill to Cardiff. Nottingham-Cardiff time-tabled trains began to be worked by 170s on 22nd May.

2001

21st May : New service to London from a station on the OWW line, as Chiltern Railways extend some peak hour Snow Hill-Marylebone trains to/from Stourbridge Junction. All trains worked by Class 168 Clubman dmus. Route learning trips for Chiltern crews in a 'heritage' single unit bubble car, far as Hartlebury. This allowed for a knowledge of the road in line with plans to extend the service to Kidderminster, where the box is switched out in the late evenings, so trains terminating there have to continue to Hartlebury to cross over.

14th November : Kingswinford Junction box destroyed, replaced with ground frame.

2002

5th May : Special train, a Thames Turbo Class 166 unit, runs from Stourbridge Junction to Evesham and back to celebrate the 150th anniversary of the opening of this part of the line. Replica GWR nameboard unveiled at Pershore.

47 581, in RES livery, passes Combe with the summer Sundays 10.05 Poole-Glasgow Central, 4th July 1993. By this date locomotive hauled trains were only seen in normal service on Sundays. *(Stephen Widdowson)*

Thames Turbo 166 212 waits to depart from Evesham with the 14.05 150th Anniversary back to Stourbridge Junction, 5th May 2002.
(Stephen Widdowson)

Change, Contraction and Closure

So far as this final chapter is concerned, modern times began in December 1961, with the announcement that the Wolverhampton-Worcester line was to close to passengers between Priestfield and Stourbridge Junction. Steam still held sway on long distance trains, local goods yards remained busy and the OWW main line was intact.

Services north of Stourbridge had been thin for many years, although Wolverhampton-Worcester locals were often pulled by express passenger types on a running-in turn, freshly overhauled at Stafford Road. The last train, driven by Herbert Lawrence and fired by Cliff Totney, both of Stourbridge shed, was the 10.05pm Low Level-Stourbridge Junction on Sunday 29th July 1962. John Dew was a passenger on this train and he recalled the cacophony of sound inside Dudley tunnel when it passed the last train in the other direction, the 9.55pm from Stourbridge Junction, with many blasts of the whistle. The "Express & Star" (30th July) reported, *This is one of the services which is being discontinued owing to the fact that they are used to only a fraction of their capacity."* [The same edition described the opening of the first section of the M5 that day (junctions 4-8), and the four mile long jam at the northern end as holidaymakers queued to drive onto it.] Eight of the nine intermediate stations were closed, Dudley remaining open for other services. The Dudley-Old Hill peak hour trains, worked by Class 122 'bubble cars' after 1962, expired in 1964. Local services based on Birmingham Snow Hill had been dieselised and run at regular intervals since 1957 but this was of no benefit to Wolverhampton-Stourbridge or Dudley-Old Hill locals.

The Oxford-Worcester line was the last route out of Paddington to retain steam-hauled expresses. Western Region diesel hydraulic 'Hymeks' began arriving at Worcester in May 1963, and several months of teething troubles resulted in a stay of execution for Worcester's remaining "Castles", down to three by the autumn. One of these, 7005 "Sir Edward Elgar", was in charge of the last steam "Cathedrals Express" from Hereford to Paddington on 4th September 1963. This loco, formerly "Lamphrey Castle", had been named in honour of the Worcestershire composer in the centenary year of his birth, 1957. Also that year the 07.45 Hereford-Paddington was named "Cathedrals Express", with Mark 1 stock in Great Western chocolate and cream. Between Worcester and Oxford, it initially stopped only at Evesham and Moreton. The name was abandoned in 1965, revived 1985-97 and again briefly in 1999. The office block which blots the landscape in front of Shrub Hill, erected in 1962, was named "Elgar House" although how such a monstrosity could be a tribute to the composer, or anyone else, is hard to imagine.

The last steam local train arrived at Worcester, from Birmingham, on 4th September 1964 and the summer time-table for the following year brought an end to through Kidderminster portions for Paddington trains. Through services between Paddington, Oxford, Worcester and Wolverhampton had withered to one train in each direction by 1959, and the Kidderminster portion of the "Cathedrals Express" was a last remnant of this historic service. From now on, anyone travelling on the OWW route would have a break of journey at Worcester Shrub Hill (More recent short-lived experiments, a peak hour Birmingham-Evesham train and a Birmingham-Worcester-Paddington turbo dmu, hardly count).

The earliest diesels went the way of steam, as ex-Great Western railcars were withdrawn from Worcester and Kidderminster sheds in 1962. They had been pioneers in their day, just three units revolutionising the Birmingham-Gloucester-Cardiff express service in 1934, with subsequent cars soon put to work on local workings between Oxford, Worcester and Hereford, as well as quieter backwaters like the Severn Valley line and its branch to Tenbury Wells. Worcester, with up to seven units, always had a greater allocation than any other shed. Birmingham-Cardiff diesels began running once more in 1958, operated by Class 120 Swindon-built 'Cross Country' dmus and routed over the OWW between Stourbridge and Worcester.

As the steam era drew to a close, it played a part at the end of the life of one of the greatest Englishmen. On Saturday 30th January 1965, Sir Winston Churchill's funeral train brought his body from Waterloo to Handborough, for burial in the churchyard at Blaydon, a mile from the station and close to his birthplace at Blenheim Palace. The locomotive could only be Battle of Britain Class 4-6-2 No.34051 "Winston Churchill", originally shedded at Salisbury (72B), which was brought out of storage and moved to Nine Elms (70A) for preparation. The train consisted of five Pullman cars for mourners and a bogie van conveying the coffin. The Southern Region disc headcode was a special V for victory. The hand picked train crew, accompanied by an inspector, consisted of driver Alf Hurley, Jamie Lester, a fireman aged 22 and W. H. Horwill, guard. *"At stations all along the route hundreds of people had bought platform tickets, simply to stand with heads bared and bowed as the train passed"* ('Sunday Express', 31st January). At Reading a pilot driver stepped onto the footplate and indicated that he would drive for the rest of the journey, but the inspector, Bill Neal, insisted that the Southern driver would continue to drive throughout. Whilst Western drivers occasionally worked on Southern locomotives they did not handle Pullman rolling stock, which had a distinctive brake valve requiring a degree of handling expertise.

It had been planned to run the train at line speed through Oxford but the train crew had been advised that the city's bells would ring muffled peals as they passed through, so they slowed to 20 mph. On an earlier route learning trip - almost unheard of for a fireman - Jamie had noticed that Handborough was in a dilapidated condition, with peeling paintwork. On the day of the funeral he saw that its defects had been skilfully disguised with purple drapes.

Between Churchill's death and the funeral, which had been planned in minute detail for years, a temporary emergency facing crossover was inserted at Handborough, so that the funeral train could gain access to the up platform. The Joint Special Notice No. 41 AGM, issued by the assistant general managers of the Southern and Western regions on 26th January, stated, *"At Handborough the private special train must be brought to a stand with the centre of the engine footplate opposite a point indicated by distinctive white posts with white lights situated each side of the Up Main Line to indicate the place at which the train must stop. The distance from the centre of the engine footplate to the centre of the leading door of Bogie Van No. 2464 through which the bearer party with the coffin will alight is as follows – 99 feet 5 inches".*

After the mourners had left the station, the stock was temporarily removed from the platform by a diesel locomotive, releasing 34051, which then returned light engine to Nine Elms, the pilotman driving as far as Reading, after which Jamie Lester took charge. This was the inspector's way of thanking him for his skilled firing, as the 80 mile trip, without a planned water stop before Oxford on the return journey, was almost at the limit for the loco's 4,500 gallon tender.

Sir Winston Churchill's funeral train arriving at Handborough, 30th January 1965. *(Jamie Lester collection)*

A pair of pannier tanks, 9610 and 9630, head north through Bilston with an OWW line special, July 1965, shortly before the line closed to all traffic. *(Brian Robbins)*

The Beeching Report envisaged an accelerated express service between Oxford and Worcester, and the closure of all stations inbetween except Kingham, Moreton, Honeybourne, Evesham and Pershore. A closure proposal for the others was published in 1964. In 1965 the Minister of Transport agreed to closure of the halts west of Moreton but, apart from Adlestrop, rejected closure of those to the east 'for the time being'. He also refused consent for the closure of Charlbury. At the same time, Worcester-Paddington expresses were accelerated to 2 hours 15 mins (good, but five minutes slower than the fastest train in 1905), they ran every two hours and were hauled by brand new Class 47s. Later, when the line attracted grant aid, under the terms of the 1968 Act, it needed only £63,000 in 1970, £13,000 less than in 1969, indicating that, despite an uncertain future, it was attracting more passengers.

General freight persisted into the 1960s, and a little beyond. Yards closed as traffic declined, although Kidderminster hung on until 1983 and the coal sidings at Droitwich lasted until 1989. The yard at Stourbridge Junction had lain disused for many years when it briefly acted as a stabling point for the stock of the Galton Junction-Stourbridge resignalling scheme in 1990. The OWW north of Dudley closed to all traffic in 1965 and the track was lifted although, in contrast, Dudley Freightliner Terminal flourished for a while.

With the exception of steel, locally generated specific freight flows, still significant in 1960, had all but vanished ten years later. In September 1964 a railway carriage, specially fitted to display the products of Carpet Trades Ltd., began a promotional tour of the country, visiting 31 towns and cities before returning to Kidderminster on 23rd December. Alveley Colliery still required four trains a day. Sadly, one of them was in collision with a car on the ungated crossing at Northwood in August 1964 and two people in the car were killed. The Brierley Crystal works, adjacent to the main line, received raw materials for glass making, silver sand and potash, by rail and the finished product was dispatched in special containers. When an improved type of container had been developed in the 1930s, it was apparently 'tested' by being deliberately dropped from the bridge over the line near the factory. The contents was unscathed, a fact mentioned by both the GWR and Brierley Crystal in subsequent trade publicity. Round Oak steel works closed in 1982; its internal rail system had boasted a stud of 20 locomotives and over a thousand wagons in 1948.

The once extensive facilities at Worcester were decimated during the 1960s, with the closure of the works, repair shop and engine sheds, and the gutting of the sheet shops by fire. These had once produced the bulk of the tarpaulin sheets on the GWR, used for covering goods in short wheelbase open wagons. The Vinegar branch gathered rust and the five acre works of McKenzie & Holland, once employing 600 men and world famous for producing signalling equipment was, by this time, only a distant memory. North of Oxford, the once busy freight link between the OWW and the ex-LNWR line at Yarnton saw its last train in November 1965.

The prospects for passenger traffic seemed little better. The ex-OWW station at Stoke Works closed in 1965, to be followed later by singling of the line from Droitwich. By 1970 every branch off the OWW, apart from the Stourbridge Town and Extension lines, had closed to passengers. Main line services were also being pruned and some former stations, such as Norton, reduced to halts, but this was merely a stay of execution. Fernhill Heath and Cutnall Green closed in 1965. Cutnall Green, which had a change of name from 'Hampton Lovett' prior to opening in 1928, had 100 foot long platforms, a siding, a weighbridge for domestic coal and cost £2,280. In contrast, two single platform

halts on the Severn Valley line, Burlish built in 1930, and Jackfield built in 1934, cost £430 and £192 respectively. Burlish, unlike some minor halts, had electric lighting from its opening.

In January 1966 eight stations and halts were closed east of Worcester. Today, almost the only evidence that any of them ever existed can be found at Adlestrop, where a station nameboard is mounted in a shelter in the centre of the village. Five halts in Oxfordshire were spared, albeit with a very sparse train service. The remaining stations between Stratford and Honeybourne had closed in 1966 and, three years later, the few remaining Stratford-Worcester trains were axed and Honeybourne closed. Since enlargement of the junction and opening of the main line to Cheltenham in 1906, that station had boasted four through platforms. The junction had at one time been controlled by no fewer than six manual boxes, their signals requiring sufficient lamp oil and general care as to keep two lads fully employed. When the Stratford-Worcester trains were withdrawn, the Minister of Transport, Barbara Castle, had refused consent for the closure of Pershore which, almost as an act of petty spite, immediately had its 'service' reduced to one train a day in each direction. (Neither Pershore nor Honeybourne were proposed for closure in the Beeching Report.)

1971 was a black year for the OWW line for three reasons. January saw the start of track rationalisation at Worcester, when one side of the 'Worcester triangle', used by Hereford-Birmingham trains by-passing Shrub Hill, was singled. This was as nothing compared to the rest of the scheme, carried out two years later and as welcome as a boa constrictor's hug for the effect it had - and continues to have - on train movements. The double track between Shrub Hill and Henwick, over a mile away on the Hereford line, was converted to two parallel single tracks through Foregate Street station, one to/from Shrub Hill the other to/from the Droitwich line. Whenever there is a late running train through this bottleneck it can have serious consequences on all Worcester services. During the conversion the old low-tech lower quadrant semaphore signals were replaced - by new low-tech lower etc....... For several weeks there was severe disruption which, as a commuter, I experienced first hand, arriving late for work on most days. At a time when modern power signalling was becoming the norm over much of the network, this scheme suggested that Worcester was seen by British Rail as a backwater unworthy of serious attention.

Secondly, this impression was reinforced in the autumn of 1971 when singling of the Worcester-Oxford 'Cotswold Line', first proposed in 1967, was carried out. With effect from 25th October the $28\frac{3}{4}$ miles between Norton Junction and Moreton had just one passing loop, at Evesham. The line is worked with an electric token system, trains having to stop at Evesham box for token exchange, a fascinating ritual on the Severn Valley Railway but not appropriate for any modern line. (At least the Norton token can be exchanged at Shrub Hill as required.) Wolvercot Junction to Ascott-under-Wychwood was also singled, leaving just ten miles of double track from there to Moreton. Cotswold Line freight had been dwindling and singling did nothing to slow its extinction. Bulk fertiliser traffic to Moreton (for ICI at Chipping Norton) lasted a while longer and general wagonload freight continued at Evesham until 1981.

Thirdly, with the start of the new time-table, on 4th May 1971, the all day semi-fast service, Birmingham-Worcester-Hereford via Stourbridge, was withdrawn outside the peak hours. The Kidderminster-Droitwich section now only saw passenger trains in the peak hours. The track remained double, signalling was not tampered with, but the service was torn to shreds. Straightforward journeys, such as Worcester-Stourbridge or Kidderminster-Malvern, were impossible for most of the day.

60 015 is signalled into the loop at the rear of Shrub Hill station as it approaches Worcester Tunnel with a Round Oak-Margam steel train, 12th June 1997.

(David Gomersall)

This 'Droitwich gap' remained in the time-table for twelve years. In the meantime, Kidderminster was at the end of a virtual branch line from Birmingham New Street, with an hourly all-stations train taking 42 minutes to cover 18 miles.

Ever since the 1850s the former joint station at Shrub Hill had had some long distance expresses to such places as Bristol, Derby and York. These InterCity trains, as they were successfully branded in modern times, all by-passed Worcester, reverting to the 'old line' via Spetchley, after May 1981. As main line speeds increased with the introduction of High Speed Trains (HSTs) in October 1982, and as Bristol-Birmingham trains had up to twenty minutes added to their schedules when using the Worcester loop, calls at Shrub Hill were seen as less and less commercially viable. An alternative, a two-level Worcester Parkway station on the outskirts of the city, where the Cotswold Line bridges the Bristol-Birmingham line, was first unveiled in plans made public on 12th January 1977. Exactly a year later the £1 million scheme, <u>which would also have meant the closure of Shrub Hill to passengers</u>, was agreed by British Rail and Hereford & Worcester County Council. There were to be 22 HSTs calling at Worcester Parkway daily, and the North East-South West Inter City route (now Virgin Cross Country) was to be worked exclusively by HSTs. However, the full fleet of HSTs was not ordered because there was a shortfall in government funding. The full service could not be provided and the scheme was abandoned. More recent attempts to revive Parkway, none of them successful, have not suggested the closure of Shrub Hill, so there has been progress of a sort since 1977.

Progress and Revival

Since the late 1970s there has been, on balance, more 'progress and revival' than 'contraction and closure', although it has often been a case of "two steps forward and one back". One small sign of positive thinking, which proved to be a straw in the wind, occurred in 1975, when the train service at Pershore was doubled, bringing the daily total to four. The extras were a 10.32 to Worcester, with a return calling at 14.29, although it was still not possible to travel to Evesham and back on the same day! The improvement followed a short campaign by the local branch of the Railway Invigoration Society (forerunner of the Railway Development Society) supported by people living near the station in Pinvin, and listened to by sympathetic rail management. When the new Worcester-bound train stopped on the first day, six people got on and a student from Oxford got off, asking about a bus connection to the town centre, a mile and a half away. Pershore station's fortunes have improved steadily since then, so that most trains call there, seven days a week, except the Monday-Friday HSTs operated by First Great Western. The bus link to the town centre began in 1986.

The five Oxfordshire halts - Shipton, Ascott, Finstock, Combe, Handborough - had the same level of service as Pershore. It was improved briefly, without success, in 1974, but the potential of Handborough (now spelt without the 'd') was recognised soon after and the number of trains stopping there gradually increased. The level of service is now as good, and to the same pattern, as at Pershore. In consequence, Hanborough is busy throughout the day, with a morning flow of commuters into Oxford, some continuing to Paddington. The halt is on a confined site, near a small industrial estate and a bus museum, with little obvious scope for a much needed expansion to the rail users' car park, 25 spaces for about 40 cars on most days. The rail journey to Oxford takes 10 minutes, as opposed to forty by car in the peak. Oxford City Council actively discourages car journeys into the city and there are large and efficient park and ride sites on the outskirts. People using local stations, including Hanborough, can buy a carnet of Thames Trains tickets, ten for the price of nine, which can be used as required, not necessarily on ten consecutive weekdays. Despite the inadequate car park, Hanborough has a wide catchment area, some people driving in from Witney.

Finstock and Combe are in delightful country which is largely devoid of people. Regular daily users are numbered in single figures. It would have been better had the GWR followed its original intention in the 1930s, by building just one halt on this part of the line, to serve the larger village of Stonesfield. Finstock and Combe were under notice of closure as recently as 1994. They were reprieved, but their short platforms can only be used by two-car turbos. The only westbound train of the day which called at all the halts had, for many years, left Oxford around 17.25. Passenger numbers grew to the extent that there were sometimes as many as eighty people standing as far as Moreton, but no more than four or five travelling to Combe or Finstock. It was decided, with the agreement of the Strategic Rail Authority, to lengthen this train to three cars and omit stops at Combe, Finstock and Ascott, which would be served instead by the less crowded 18.28 from Oxford. As Terry Worrall, General Manager of Thames Trains, explained in conversation, *"It is inconvenient for a very small number of people but a great benefit, in our view, for a much larger number"*. The cost of lengthening the platforms at Combe and Finstock by one coach length each, together with the Railway Inspectorate requirement of bringing the existing platforms up to the same standard as the extensions, has been estimated by Railtrack at about £600,000, which is a prohibitive figure plucked from the realms of fantasy. The cost of restrospectively fitting current rolling stock with conductor controlled selective door opening - so that only doors alongside a platform can open - is also prohibitive. Such technology is available, but only practical when built into new stock, therefore it is not a short term solution. Meanwhile, Shipton now has a slightly improved, if lopsided service, with one train to and four from Oxford; Finstock and Ascott are both served, additionally, by the bus link from Charlbury. (North of Worcester, the much busier halt at Blakedown had its three-car platforms lengthened in 1994; as longer Sprinter trains became the norm on the Birmingham line during the peaks the investment was considered worthwhile.)

In addition to Pershore and Hanborough, Honeybourne is another successfully revived station. It reopened as a halt, using part of what was the down main line platform. During preparatory work an overweight lorry backed onto the platform, tipping its load. This created a bulge in the platform side, fouling the loading gauge. The signalman at Moreton, where a train was about to depart for Worcester, was contacted immediately. The train did not leave and disaster was narrowly avoided. The damaged section of platform, at the Worcester end, was removed and not replaced. The station, reopened on an experimental basis from 25th May 1981 until the following October, has about the same level of service as Pershore and Hanborough. Whilst Honeybourne had been closed a maximum security prison was built nearby at Long Lartin. The permanent staff of about 250 and their families, plus visitors for the prisoners, generate useful custom for the railway and local taxi firms.

The Honeybourne reopening was an early cause for celebration by the Cotswold Line Promotion Group (CLPG). The group had been formed in 1978 by a number of rail users keen to see the Cotswold Line, as it had officially been labelled in 1974, maximise its potential. They were not aware of any threat to the line (but see below), neither were they demanding any kind of instant action. About ninety people were at the inaugural meeting in Moreton. Two Moreton residents, Oliver Lovell and Alfred Fountain, were key figures in the group's formation and, even before that first meeting, had approached BR management saying they wished to work with them in a spirit of co-operation whenever possible. The words 'Promotion Group' - rather than 'Action Group', which can imply a certain militancy - were well chosen and the group quickly won the respect of railway professionals, which it has kept ever since. A CLPG presence was established very early on, with posters, leaflets, etc., at stations along the route. Committee members have always acted rather like a neighbourhood watch, as they are rail users with a personal interest in their local station or halt who can be contacted by ordinary members (current membership stands at about 1,800). There have been many improvements on the line since 1978, some of which would not have come about as they did had it not been for the CLPG.

There have also been disappointments, cutbacks and rumours of cutbacks. Of the rumours, a senior BR manager made it known some years after the event, that even as the group was being formed, serious official consideration was being given to an 'economy measure' to sever the line and operate it as two branches, Worcester-Evesham and Oxford-Moreton!

In January 1981, and again in May 1982, even as Honeybourne reopened and Pershore started to prosper, real and serious cutbacks were proposed by BR. Paddington-Worcester-Hereford trains, at that time all loco-hauled, were to be diverted via Swindon and Cheltenham and replaced between Oxford and Worcester by diesel multiple units which were twenty years old and showing their age. The reason for this was given by BR staff when questioned at the CLPG's annual general meeting in May 1981. It was the poor state of about seven miles of jointed wooden-sleepered track, mostly between Ascott and Wolvercot, which needed replacing urgently at a cost of £1.5 million (which would, at the time, have repaired about a mile and a half of motorway). It now seems incredible that BR, working with a severely restricted cashflow imposed by H.M.Treasury, had to contemplate virtually destroying the train service for the sake of £1.5 million. Sir Peter Parker, Chairman of BR at the time and a regular commuter from Charlbury, once famously criticised the lack of political will to invest in Britain's railways as being responsible for their "crumbling edge of quality", and this was exactly the sort of thing he meant. The CLPG distributed over 6,000 leaflets, in which it set out the harsh facts, without blaming British Rail -

"CLPG sympathises fully with British Rail over their financial plight, for they are in desperate need of more Government support. Nevertheless, an alternative to the withdrawal plan MUST be found. The Group has suggested, as a compromise, that some off-peak through trains could be replaced by dmus, thus reducing costs and prolonging the life of the track ...". Committee members and others spent countless hours organising meetings, writing letters, enlisting support and listening to the BR point of view. Local MPs added their own soundbites to the debate and the story featured on the television news. An article in "Modern Railways Insight" (a supplement to 'Modern Railways', published autumn 1981), entitled "Oxford-Worcester: The first Inter-City Victim?", described the problems besetting the line with great clarity. It also highlighted the increase in passengers between 1977 and 1979, attributing much of it to the hard work and effectiveness of the CLPG. Annual figures at

Pershore station, with flower areas maintained by volunteers from the Cotswold Line Promotion Group, presents a basic but neat appearance as Sprinter 150 270, in Regional Railways livery, arrives with the 14.16 Hereford-Oxford, 30th March 1989.

(Stephen Widdowson)

The basic facilities at Honeybourne, soon after reopening, with an Oxford bound train.

(Brian Robbins)

Charlbury climbed from 65,494 to 81,152; Kingham 31,258 - 36,615; Moreton 56,370 - 68,193; Evesham 114,645 - 130,198. (In 2001 passenger figures for Evesham exceeded a quarter of a million.)

A compromise solution was reached, as suggested by CLPG, keeping two loco hauled morning trains to Paddington and two evening returns, with all other Cotswold Line services run by dmus, and this has been the pattern of the now much expanded time-table ever since. Funds were eventually allocated to replace the offending track and the CLPG Newsletter (Spring 1984) remarked, *"The Cotswold Line is currently going through a period of convalescence after several years of serious illness culminating recently in several transplant operations in the form of much needed track renewal"*. The same issue also warned about possible reductions in services to Pershore and Honeybourne and advertised no fewer than seven BR Merrymaker excursions (remember them?) during the summer, plus a CLPG train to York. The line saw its first High Speed Train (HST) in May 1984, the 10.05 Paddington-Great Malvern and return. The HSTs, with lighter axle loads than locomotives, cause less wear on the track. They replaced all weekday loco-hauled trains between Oxford, Worcester and Hereford from May 1988, although some weekend workings were loco-hauled until 1993.

By this time the CLPG was also the user group for the Hereford line; its name remained unchanged but since 1986 the newsletter has been branded the "Cotswold & Malvern Line News". Earlier, in 1982, the CLPG had supported the formation of a short-lived "Birmingham Kidderminster Worcester Line Promotion Group". Worcester no longer had an InterCity service to Birmingham or Bristol by then so, as a kind of substitute, BR had improved the Birmingham-Worcester local service via Bromsgrove. The station there had had only one platform since 1969, trains to Worcester having to cross to 'wrong road' at the foot of the Lickey Incline when calling. This was beginning to cause operational difficulties as the number of HSTs on the route increased and no one, as yet, had found a way of funding a second platform (it eventually opened in May 1990, paid for by the county council). Most local trains were therefore removed from the Bromsgrove line and rerouted via Stourbridge, where the whole service was recast, from May 1983. The Kidderminster-Droitwich gap was plugged, some trains were semi-fast and the line was open on Sundays for the first time since 1965. Overnight, this became the best ever local service between Worcester, Kidderminster and Birmingham and the line's Promotion Group soon ceased to exist, having achieved everything it wanted, almost without asking. It was later succeeded by the Stourbridge Line User Group which, among other things, is keen to see restoration of the passenger service on the remaining part of the OWW north of Stourbridge, to Dudley, and from there to Walsall and beyond.

The Birmingham-Stourbridge-Worcester service has grown considerably since 1983. There are two trains per hour, most going through to Great Malvern, half providing an hourly link with Hereford. Until 2002 it was dominated by the basic Class 150 Sprinters, but Class 156 and 158 units are increasingly to be seen.

Worcester Shrub Hill has had long distance 'non Inter City' trains since May 1987, when a two-hourly Birmingham-Cardiff service via Stourbridge began. In May 1990, with the provision of Bromsgrove's second platform, these trains transferred to that route. Now operated by Central Trains, the service has since been extended to Derby and Nottingham. Some trains by-pass Worcester, using the 'old road' via Spetchley, as do all the Birmingham-Cardiff dmus operated by Wales & Borders Trains.

In 2001, Central Trains attempted to further increase Worcester's range of destinations by seeking to provide a Birmingham-Worcester-Bristol service. The bid was successfully opposed by Virgin Cross Country, on the grounds that it would be unfair competition, arguing that there were enough trains on the route already. Yes, but all are operated by Virgin Cross Country and none call at Worcester.

Between Oxford and Worcester, the two main trains of the day to/from Paddington are handled by First Great Western HSTs. Other Cotswold Line services are operated by Thames Trains and employ Class 165 and 166 units. There is now a more frequent service than ever before. It cannot run at regular intervals, because of the long sections of single track. Nevertheless, summer 2002 saw 15 down and 14 up weekday trains between Oxford and Worcester, all but one in each direction going through to/from Paddington, an improvement brought about by Thames Trains in May 1998. Three trains each way are operated by First Great Western, the remainder by Thames Trains. The 09.48 Paddington-Hereford and the 13.04 return is one of the FGW trains, yet it looks like a Thames turbo, it is a Thames turbo. As Terry Worrall explained, *"It's a First Great Western service, we provide the unit, they provide the crew"*.

All but one train in each direction also serve Worcester Foregate Street, some continuing to Great Malvern or Hereford. As the Hereford line is single for over 17 miles between Malvern Wells and Shelwick Junction, with a passing loop at Ledbury, timetabling Oxford-Worcester-Hereford trains is more complex than on other, busier lines which have the luxury of uninterrupted double track.

Terry Worrall recalled the Cotswold line in the late 1970s when there were fewer trains (eight in each direction in the 1978-79 time-table) and, given the increased number of trains with the same infrastructure, *"we are now at absolute capacity with what we can currently run to the existing stopping patterns"*. No new stations have opened on the line since Honeybourne in 1981, although there has been a campaign for a station at Chipping Campden, and there are still hopes for Worcester Parkway. Apart from the cost of building even one of these stations, the time taken for trains to call there would have serious implications for the whole time-table on this single track at-capacity line.

There have been several recent capacity studies, notably the Five Counties Study in 2000, to which Thames Trains and Railtrack both contributed. It investigated what might be achieved with differing levels of investment, ranging from redoubling the whole line (£100 million) to appreciable capacity improvements for half that sum or less. One possibility is redoubling the five miles between Norton and Pershore, which would allow greater flexibility of working and enable the off-peak time-table to operate at regular, hourly intervals - readily understood, easily remembered, user-friendly and likely to attract more passengers. It would also be relatively inexpensive to install a reversing facility at Foregate Street for trains from Shrub Hill, by signalling that part of the line for bi-directional running, thus eliminating the need for trains to trundle over the river to Henwick in order to reverse. Such aspirations must take account of needs and demands elsewhere on the network. Funding will be in the gift of the Strategic Rail Authority and their most recent ten year plan does not envisage substantial expenditure on the Cotswold line.

As recently as 1998 the freight company EWS expressed an interest in a railhead in the Vale of Evesham, at either Evesham or Honeybourne. Such a scheme, though desirable, has little chance of happening until line capacity is improved.

It has long been recognised that the Worcester area signalling and track layout is in need of modernisation. A scheme was

Class 158s cross at Shrub Hill with 158 850 on the 12.42 Nottingham-Cardiff and 158 785 on the 12.54 Cardiff-Nottingham. The units are in pristine condition and even have bi-lingual destination displays. A heritage bubble car sulks on the middle road. 20th March 1992.

(Stephen Widdowson)

166 203 arrives at Evesham with an Oxford-Worcester crew training trip on 3rd May 1993, prior to the introduction of these units into passenger service over the Cotswold Line later that month.

(Stephen Widdowson)

begun in the winter of 1989/90 and colour light signals were installed, but never activated, on the approach to Shrub Hill. Despite the negative experience of too much single track on the Cotswold line, and between Shrub Hill and Henwick, and despite increased use of the line, the scheme actually involved more single track. Norton Junction was to be abolished as a junction, with two parallel single tracks, one for the OWW, one for the Gloucester line, between there and Shrub Hill. A change in local management in 1990 brought the realisation that this would render the Cotswold line time-table virtually unworkable, so the scheme was abandoned and the signals removed. Any new scheme, which would be funded by Railtrack, would only be of benefit between Oxford and Worcester in conjunction with an improvement in track capacity.

The OWW is controlled from twelve traditional signal boxes - Ascott, Moreton, Evesham, Worcester Shrub Hill, Worcester Tunnel Junction, Droitwich, Hartlebury, Kidderminster, Blakedown, Stourbridge Junction, Kingswinford Junction - although some have outgrown their traditional role and most have lost their traditional appearance with the installation of double glazing. The last mentioned box has lost any kind of appearance at all, as it was destroyed in an arson attack in November 2001 and has since been replaced on site with a ground frame. Stourbridge Junction is a power signalling panel box, controlling train movements on the Extension as far as Galton Junction. Droitwich, Shrub Hill and Moreton, still manual boxes, are all equipped with 'TRUST', a computer system which details the condition of trains due to pass through the area. The signaller can bring onto the screen a variety of information about each train, its type, time-keeping, make-up. Each train's consist is coded (eg; 41 is a 1st class HST car, 42 is 2nd class, 43 a power car, etc.). The information is keyed into TRUST manually at each train's originating station or freight depot. It is possible to determine the time keeping of specific trains at specific locations over a period of a week. The working time-table can also be called up a week in advance, very useful for occasional freight workings (such as to Round Oak or Brierley Hill steel terminals) and for specials.

Feeder buses were encouraged by the CLPG, in an effort to reach the parts a railway would not normally reach. They are now an established and successful feature, many running regularly throughout the day, with stops at the stations. Some are listed on the station nameboards and in this regard "Moreton-in-Marsh, change here for buses to Chipping Campden, Stow-on-the-Wold and Bourton-on-the-Water" must be of record length for this type of information. Oxford station has bus stands on the forecourt. During the 1990s, services were operated by electric vehicles which 'plugged in' at the stands, recharging batteries between duties. Other bus links operate from Charlbury (to Finstock, Leafield, Ascott), Kingham (to Chipping Norton), Evesham (to/from Moreton via Broadway and Chipping Campden) Pershore (town centre), Kidderminster (Bewdley, Stourport, Areley Kings). Stourbridge Town is next to the bus station. Thames Trains also encourages feeder buses, working closely with the bus operators and county councils in an effort to integrate bus and train. As Terry Worrall remarked, *"we are keen to see integration work and that it represents good value for money"*. In 2001 Thames Trains launched a rail/bus ticket for Worcester, valid on trains and the city's local buses, which has proved successful, with about 8% of rail passengers to Worcester buying them.

Since the 1980s, due to the improved train services, there has been a dramatic increase in the number of passengers driving to stations. Stourbridge Junction now has five trains per hour to Birmingham, two to Worcester and a service to London

Marylebone. Unsurprisingly, the 250 space free car park is frequently full by 9am and there are plans to extend it by 144 spaces. Visitors to the Severn Valley Railway share the car park at Kidderminster, also using other areas nearby on busy weekends. At Droitwich, commuters' cars spill out from the station area onto the adjoining roads. Shrub Hill's 50 spaces are often all occupied after the departure of the two FGW trains to Paddington. On the Cotswold line, Thames Trains operates the stations and their car parks. It is often expensive to provide more spaces, in terms of both money and land. Terry Worrall noted, *"at some stations, expansion usually means going upwards rather than outwards, but in a rural area a multi-storey car park would not be seen as a solution. At some stations there is land, but it is not always available or usable."* The car park at Evesham (75 spaces) urgently needs expanding. There is potential for an extra site on the other side of the line but it would require considerable earthworks, drainage, extra lighting, etc. The station sees over 800 passengers journeys per weekday and there is even a small band of daily London commuters, 106 miles from Paddington (an annual season ticket cost £4,872 in 2002). Charlbury attracts commuters to Oxford and Paddington and its 150 space car park is usually overflowing at the end of the morning peak, not surprising when there are over 900 passenger journeys a day here. *"There is a hole outside the station on top of which we could provide a 90 space car park, but the hole, which also has a drainage function, would cost £600,000 to fill in"*. Before such improvements are undertaken it is not so much the actual cost that Thames Trains has to consider, but rather their cost effectiveness - will they give value for money? Kingham car park was extended from 100 to 150 spaces in 2002.

Many stations have been rebuilt, refurbished or otherwise improved in recent years. The booking hall at Shrub Hill provides an attractive entrance to the station, Evesham is 'Great Western smart' in appearance if not in colour scheme, and an original well maintained OWW building is Charlbury's focal point. Kingham's old buildings were replaced in 1981 but the well kept station is still a good place at which to end a train journey. Some halts have been improved too, notably Pershore, with its seat in memory of Jack Fowles, recognising his many years of voluntary work in maintaining the station. In 2002, Pershore was provided with a replica GWR nameboard to mark the 150th anniversary of the opening of the line. North of Worcester however, replacement buildings were not so kind to Kidderminster in the 1960s, nor, in the 1970s to Droitwich, once noted for its gardens which boasted busts of Roman gods, a thatched summerhouse and the station name picked out in rustic. In my view, the best rebuilding, which is in the OWW title if not on the line, is at Oxford. Opened in 1990, it is the first permanent station on the site. Its predecessors, although lasting a permanent number of years, were intended as temporary, and pretty miserable they were too. Oxford today is modern, light, easy to use, although diesel fumes help to make the light brickwork at platform level look rather grubby. Automatic ticket barriers, with staff in attendance, ensure that only legitimate travellers are allowed onto the platforms, an important consideration, especially at night, or if you are a woman, or travelling alone. It is an obvious safety feature which has been allowed to lapse at many large stations in recent years......

North of Stourbridge, the OWW remains double track, used by Class 60 and 66 locos on steel trains to Brierley Hill and Round Oak. The line beyond, to Dudley and Walsall, closed as a through route to freight in 1993, although some track remains on the overgrown formation. There are proposals, supported by the railfreight company EWS, to reopen this line, which would relieve congestion on other freight routes in the West Midlands. It would also have a passenger service, linking Worcester, Stourbridge, Dudley, Walsall, Lichfield and Derby. At the time of writing there seems to be a conflict of interest between promoters of a reopened railway and Midland Metro, who plan an extension along part of the route, between Wednesbury and Brierley Hill. There is not room for each to have continuous double track, shared track would be unworkable and neither party wants an undue amount of single track. North of Dudley this disused line leaves the OWW, curving north-east towards Walsall as the South Staffordshire railway.

The OWW once continued north, behind what is now the Black Country Living Museum. Track was lifted after the discontinuance of freight in 1965. Although the trackbed has since become largely submerged under housing and light industrial estates, it remains easy to trace on a current A-Z map, as it still forms the district council boundary as far as Bilston. At Priestfield it emerges for a brief 500 metres or so, as part of Line 1 of Midland Metro, which then turns along Bilston Road to reach the centre of Wolverhampton, leaving a last weed-choked remnant of trackbed to find its way to the Low Level station.

Since May 2001 it has again been possible to catch a London train from an OWW station north of Worcester. Chiltern Railways augmented their Snow Hill-Marylebone service by starting four morning peak trains from Stourbridge Junction, with a balancing service in the evenings. This was the beginning of a step by step improvement, eventually providing an hourly service between Kidderminster and Marylebone.......

For an overview of how the railway has changed in the time covered by this chapter, I talked to John Carter, a senior conductor with Thames Trains, in January 2002, just before his retirement. He began work as a porter at Plymouth Millbay in 1957, transferred to shunting work before coming to Worcester as a freight guard in 1960. As he explained, *"If you were a freight shunter the next step up was to become a freight guard."* The railway still carried all types of wagonload traffic. Some trains had unofficial names, such as the early morning fitted freight, which conveyed perishables, from Royal Oak (Paddington) to Worcester. It was known as 'The Panic' and anything slower in its path had to 'go back inside', into loops or sidings to let it pass. It arrived at Worcester about 5 am and its contents was offloaded manually and distributed to stores in the city and surrounding area by road vehicles, the once familiar three-wheeled mechanical horses. Along with the perishables this train carried wine, spirits and

37 714 leaves Worcester Shrub Hill in the distance and heads past Metal Box with the 16.15 (SuO) Hereford-Paddington, 16th September 1990. Colour lights have been installed, the feathers on their tops indicating that this would have been the end of two parallel single tracks from Norton Junction, Gloucester line to the left, Oxford to the right.

(David Gomersall)

tobacco. John was sometimes the guard as the second leg of a night shift. Having worked a mixed freight up from Worcester's 'London yard' he would pick up 'The Panic' at Oxford's Hinksey yard and *"it would be our back working"*.

Worcester's traffic arrived from a variety of places - Round Oak, Stourbridge, Hereford, etc., and minor yards such as Bromyard. If it was to be forwarded to London, it needed to be marshalled in the London yard east of Shrub Hill. Some London trains were heavy and required banking up Campden bank by one

6692 drops off from banking duties at Dudley Tunnel, having assisted 8109 with a Round Oak train, 10th April 1964.

(Paul Dorney; Ned Williams collection)

of the locos based at Honeybourne, which would be informed of each train's needs. If the message was "banker to Campden and run through Blockley", this meant that once over the 1 : 100 Campden bank the train was capable of continuing unaided, so the banker would not be coupled up. If the message was "banker to Moreton", this heavier train needed help over Campden and the lesser 1: 151 bank towards Moreton, which stiffened to 1 : 110 through Aston Magna. The train had to stop so that the banker could be coupled to the rear, because of the falling gradient between the two banks. As a guard, John was in prime position to see the art of the banking loco crews, no more so than when ascending the Lickey, when up to four 'Jinties' would come up from behind, one by one, to join in the banking, *"they'd space themselves out, you'd look behind and could see all the bankers gradually coming up at you, they had it sussed, these guys were good and you hardly felt them coming on"*. Trains were banked up from Stourbridge to Round Oak or, on the Extension, to Rowley Regis or Langley Green, depending on the load. Coming down the steeper banks, an unfitted train came to a stand at the stop board before descending. The guard walked to the front and, as the driver moved the train slowly forward, the guard pinned down each wagon's brakes with a brake stick, 'picking the brakes up again' at the foot of the incline.

John's younger colleagues found it hard to believe that, at busy times, a round trip between Worcester and Honeybourne could take as much as twelve hours. This was at the time of year when the fruit and vegetable traffic in the Vale of Evesham was at its heaviest. Although collecting 'perishables', the pick-up goods would still have to give way to passenger traffic. The busiest places for fruit were Pershore, Fladbury, Charlton Siding, Evesham and Littleton & Badsey. Much of the fruit was sent to London, with another flow to Cardiff. Some beet trains for Kidderminster passed through Worcester. When John was rostered to be spare guard, he and a train crew would sometimes receive a message to "go to Kingham, pick up a beet train and take it to Kidderminster". On other occasions, a beet train would be left at Worcester yard, for John and crew to complete the final leg of its journey.

During the 1960s the freight *"gradually dwindled out and for a while the freight guards were doing freight and passenger work, but eventually we all became passenger guards"*. Some passenger guards had considered themselves an elite, even though the wages were the same. They did not collect fares, they looked after all the traffic in their van and sorted and distributed all the railway's internal correspondence. They knew nothing of freight working, nor did they need to, because they never worked freight trains. Then guards began to issue tickets, as more stations became unstaffed halts. For the first time they had a commercial role as well as the duty of looking after the train......

Many years on, as a senior conductor with Thames Trains, based at Worcester and working on the Cotswold line, John found that some passengers still called him 'guard'. The conductor still guards the train and is responsible for seeing it away from stations, although on Thames Trains the driver now releases the central locking on the doors. Individuals react in many ways to the conductor. Often, when buying a ticket on board, a passenger will say "return please" and wait expectantly, forgetting to say where they are going. Occasionally John has been tempted to react to passengers. Some years ago, in a dmu bound for Oxford an elderly lady said, *"Can we ask you a question, I've been arguing with my friend and she says there's no driver on this train. Is there?"* *"That's absolutely right madam, we won't go into the technicalities, but there are pieces of apparatus on the line which operate the acceleration and braking systems on the train."* John left them as the friend said, "I told you so, isn't it marvellous". The train failed at Ascott and John walked through, informing passengers that the driver had arranged for a rescue

John Carter and Jane Cranham, both senior conductors with Thames Trains. John began his railway career at Plymouth Millbay station. He retired in April 2002.   *(Stephen Widdowson collection)*

engine to come out from Oxford, at which the woman stood up and said, *"I've never been taken in like that in all my life"*.

Inevitably, there have been encounters with fare dodgers, including some who 'hide' on the rack, thinking they will not be seen. Others hide in the toilets, lurk in corners, look out of the window on a dark night, hold a newspaper close to their face or babble incessantly into a mobile phone, all in the vain hope that somehow they will blend into the background. But as John said to a young colleague in training who he had just seen walk through a carriage without spotting some of these characters, *"stop, look, observe, its all psychology and experience"*. One of the most stubborn ticketless customers he encountered was a man in a suit, travelling first class. At the time Thames Trains operated a penalty fare of £10 for such evasion. John explained politely but the suit was determined not to pay, so John wrote out a penalty fare notice and asked for a name. Suddenly the bluster collapsed as the suit, who turned out to be a lawyer, hastily said *"I'll pay"*.

John Carter experienced virtually no trouble, certainly no specific incidents that he could recall, even on late night trains. Not long before retirement he was offered the opportunity of going on a 'conflict course' at Reading but decided not to attend, as experience had taught him that a lack of confrontation on his part generally defused any awkward situations. There was the sad case of one girl, travelling alone on a late night train, who was conscious but appeared to be in a trance, not flinching when asked for her ticket. John realised she was suffering from the effects of drugs so arranged for paramedics to meet the train at Shrub Hill. Apart from a very few instances such as this, coming to work was always a pleasure especially since, in recent years, John was able to see at first hand the increasing numbers of trains and passengers on the Cotswold line.

There is also a better service than ever before between Worcester and Stourbridge, and there are long term hopes to reinstate a passenger service to Dudley. No trains will ever run on the OWW route beyond there but, apart from that, over 150 years after it opened, the Oxford Worcester & Wolverhampton Railway is alive and well.

ACKNOWLEDGEMENTS

Many people have readily offered help, advice, assistance, use of facilities, photographs, etc. in the preparation of this book. Particular thanks are due to the following -

Audie Baker	- Kidderminster Railway Museum
John Carter	- Senior Conductor, Thames Trains
Michael Hale	- railway historian
Jamie Lester	- ex-Southern Region railwayman
Oliver Lovell	- Cotswold Line Promotion Group
Gordon Park	- archive material
Robert Pearson	- archive material
Ken Werrett	- proof reading
Terry Worrall	- General Manager, Thames Trains Ltd.

Some of the above provided photographs, as did the following -
Richard Amott, R.K.Blencowe, Steve Burdett, Andrew Bell, Roger Carpenter, Michael Clemens, Hugh Davies, John Dew, Paul Dorney, John Edgington, Dave Gommersall, Michael Mensing, John Mudge, David Pagett, Jim Peden, Keith Potts, Brian Robbins, Stephen Widdowson, Ned Williams.

The author wishes to state that although he received much valuable assistance from railway staff and others working in an official capacity, any unattributable opinions expressed in the text of this book are entirely his own.

BIBLIOGRAPHY
(and related reading)

THE BANBURY AND CHELTENHAM RAILWAY 1887-1962
J.H.Russell
1984 : Oxford Publishing Co.
ISBN 0 902888 45 5

BLACK COUNTRY RAILWAYS
Ned Williams
1995 : Alan Sutton Publishing
ISBN 0 7509 0934 X

BRUNEL'S BROAD GAUGE IN THE BLACK COUNTRY
Michael Hale, author and publisher : 1997
ISBN 0 9501951 6 2

ISAMBARD KINGDOM BRUNEL , a biography
L.T.C.Rolt
1957 : Longmans Green & Co.

THE FAIRFORD BRANCH
S.C.Jenkins
1985 : Oakwood Press
ISBN 85361 316 8

GWR BRANCH LINES
C.J.Gammell : 1995 : OPC
ISBN 0 86093 521 3

AN HISTORICAL SURVEY OF SELECTED GREAT WESTERN STATIONS
R.H.Clark : 1976 : Oxford Publishing Co.
Oxford Publishing Co.
SBN 902888 29 3

A HISTORY OF THE GREAT WESTERN RAILWAY
Volume One 1833-1863 E.T.MacDermot, revised by C.R.Clinker
1964 : ISBN 0 7110 0411 0

THE OXFORD WORCESTER & WOLVERHAMPTON RAILWAY
S.C.Jenkins & H.I.Quayle
1977 : Oakwood Press

THE RAILWAYS OF STOURBRIDGE
Clive Butcher
1998 : Oakwood Press
ISBN 0 85361 533 0

RAILWAYS OF THE WEST MIDLANDS, A CHRONOLOGY 1808-1954
Ed.Charles R.Clinker : 1954
The Stephenson Locomotive Society

A REGIONAL HISTORY OF THE RAILWAYS OF GREAT BRITAIN
Volume 7, The West Midlands Rex Christiansen
1973 (and 1991) : David & Charles
ISBN 0 7153 6093 0

A REGISTER OF CLOSED PASSENGER STATIONS AND GOODS DEPOTS 1830-1970
Clinker & Firth : 1971

A REGISTER OF GREAT WESTERN RAILWAY HALTS AND PLATFORMS 1903-1975
C.R.Clinker : 1976

THE SEVERN VALLEY RAILWAY
John Marshall : 1989
David & Charles
ISBN 0 946537 45 3

THE WEST MIDLAND LINES OF THE GWR
Keith Beck : 1983
Ian Allan
ISBN 0 7110 1211 3

Various journals, newspapers and documents, acknowledged in the text.